Puppy Training

How to Housebreak Your Puppy in Just 7 Days!

Ken Phillips

DISCLAIMER

The information presented on this site is provided for informational purposes only, it is not meant to substitute for medical advice or diagnosis provided by your physician or other medical professional. Do not use this information to diagnose, treat or cure any illness or health condition. If you have, or suspect that you have a medical problem, contact your physician or health care provider.

The author and/or any of their proprietors assume no liability for any injury, illness or adverse affects caused by the misuse and/or use of the information or products presented in this book.

CONTENTS

FREE GIFT FOR MY READERS:

As way of saying thank you, I created this Beautiful
Puppy/Dog Care Planner just for You!
Keep track of your most important pet records.

- Pet Information
- Potty Training Tracker
- Vaccination Tracker
- Vet Visit Notes
- Training Log and more!

Download Now

https://www.mypuppyguru.com/PuppyPlannerLP

Or scan on your mobile:

Intro

Welcome to the great big beautiful world of dog companionship!

Getting a new puppy can be very exciting! But you don't want your new furry bundle of joy leaving not-so-joyous bundles and puddles throughout your house.

Properly teaching your pup where to do his business is a very important first step in any dog's life and a big responsibility on your part. Improperly trained dogs are one of the main reasons shelters stay full. Up to 25 percent of dogs relinquished to animal shelters by their owners end up there due to housebreaking problems.

Coming home to a mess after a hard day's work is the last thing you want to look forward to, and it can strain your relationship with your dog. The worst part is that it's not the dog's fault. You may want to blame him, but the fault is really yours. He's just doing what's natural to him.

One of the main reasons attempts to potty train fail is because pet owners tend to look at their dogs as four-legged humans. Once you understand how your dog sees the world and his natural instincts, you can use it to your advantage. The other reason house-training often fails is that owners are inconsistent in establishing and following reasonable routines. Timing is everything-especially with puppies with short digestion tracks.

By implementing the simple techniques you're about to discover in this book, you can have your pup potty trained in less than 7 days and get on to the business of enjoying your new best friend. Enjoy!

Chapter 1: Puppy Psychology 101

There is a certain joy that only puppies can bring to the family or to the independent individual looking for warmth and companionship in a bundle of fur. Ask any dog owner on your street and you'll hear how puppies can tug at your heartstrings like nothing else can.

We sometimes forget when we look at that wiggly furry ball of cuteness, that a puppy is still just a baby. Sure, he may be more capable at eight weeks of age than a human is but he still has to learn everything about his new world. He has the ability to become the dog that you've always dreamed of, but you will have to show him how to get there.

When it comes to puppies, no one talks very much about the sleepless first nights when the pup whines in his crate or the days when the owner feels like his pup will never learn to pee outside. New puppy owners can feel overwhelmed by the amount of supervision and care a young pup requires so they postpone dealing with training until later. He'll get it when he's older and smarter, right?

Sadly, it's the puppy who suffers the most in these situations. Some owners blame the pup for being 'bad' or 'stupid.' But it's not his fault. He just can't hold it — at least not for very long. A puppy under the age of 4 months doesn't have a big enough bladder to go more than a few hours without eliminating. Not only is he scolded unfairly but he is also exposed to a lot of stress. The pup can become confused and often fearful. A fearful dog is a hotbed of potential behavior problems. Plus he can also get very sick, especially if his owners don't clean up after him or teach him where and when to go potty.

So...is there a solution to this problem? Absolutely! All you have to do is follow Mother Nature's footsteps. House-training doesn't have to be a long, drawn-out, frustrating affair. Your puppy comes pre-programmed to eliminate outside his den and also to please his owner. You just need to learn how to communicate with him to teach him acceptable behavior.

When the puppies are first born, they eat and relieve themselves inside their den. The mother will quickly clean them to remove the scent of urine and feces. When the pups are old enough to wander about, she will gently nudge them outside the whelping nest with her nose anytime they indicate they need to go potty. As they get older, they learn to use areas farther outside the den as they imitate their mother. This helps to keep other animals away from the den and protect the pack.

With a young puppy, you are taking his mother's place. You need to teach him the acceptable behavior for YOUR pack. This makes the housebreaking process a good time to introduce your general house rules to a pup, as well as socialize him well enough to have a happy stable dog in the future.

Many of those new to owning a dog think that housebreaking is concerned *only* with teaching the pup not to eliminate in the house. Many other very important events are also taking place. Aside from teaching your pup the proper canine bathroom etiquette, you are also establishing your role as the pack leader.

Housebreaking is really about teaching your pup his place in your pack. So, a housebroken dog is also calm inside the house (the pack's den), will not chew on the furniture or footwear, and follows the pack's routines. He knows what he can play with, what and when he can eat, and how he should react to visitors.

A housebroken pup is a joy to be around, not because you've trained him to be a push-button dog, but because he understands the 'house rules,' and follows them willingly in order to live harmoniously with your human pack.

How long does housebreaking usually take?

The amount of time needed to house-train a pup is entirely dependent on the owner. If you implement the methods outlined in this book and are consistent, the potty training part of your pup's life can be condensed into just seven days (or less) with only occasional accidents. The time and attention that you invest in training now will give you a marvelous and dependable companion for the next ten, fifteen, or even twenty years!.

All you need to do is prepare yourself and your house thoroughly and get the necessary materials. If you put time and care into housebreaking your pup, you'll have no more mess inside a week!

What age should a puppy be housebroken?

The ideal time to housebreak a pup would begin the moment he leaves his littermates and mother and is taken to his new family's house. In other words, house-training begins the moment you bring your puppy home. Your objective is to never let him go inside your house, but you do need to accept that accidents will happen.

Most pups are between two and three months old when they are adopted. The age is regulated by state law and varies from state to state. By that time, the mother has already begun to teach the pup to eliminate outside the den, so you are just continuing that process. But little puppies have little bladders, and they don't have much control over their muscles yet. You need to remember this, and stay positive, patient, and loving. The type of bond you build with your puppy now will determine the future relationship that you share with your adult dog.

Of course, there are some pups that leave their litter when they are a little older, and some dogs are adults before they find their forever home. Depending upon the circumstances the pup or dog has been living in, housebreaking may be either easier or more challenging with an older canine. Some already understand it and just need to adapt to the new routines in your home; others, especially those who have been kept crated or kenneled, will be starting from scratch. The method for house-training, however, is the same, no matter the dog's age.

What do I need to be successful with training my pup?

The main thing that you need is *knowledge*. Read this book thoroughly before beginning the housebreaking process.

You will learn what to do, how to do it, and what items will make the whole process easier for you and your pup. You need to understand the instincts that Mother Nature has built into your dog, so that you can use those to make teaching him everything easier. You must learn how to reward him, how to make a reasonable schedule for him, and what his limitations are. Knowledge is the key to unlocking a well-housetrained dog that is a joy to live with.

Chapter 2: Viewing the World through Your Pup's Eyes

A major mistake, maybe THE major mistake that many people make when training their dogs is viewing them as four-legged humans. They're not. While we may sometimes think of them as our furry 'children,' they are *not children.* They don't think in human patterns or experience the world in the same way that we do. They do, however, adapt marvelously to living within our human routines, bringing all their best attributes to enriching our daily lives. To easily train your pup, whether it's housebreaking or any other behavior, it's important to understand how dogs view the world.

All canines, from timber wolves to Chihuahuas, are by nature social animals that live in packs. Pack mentality is hard-wired into their brains. The pack is their source of security, play, care, and food. It gives them stability and enables them to survive in nature since the pack functions as a cohesive unit. Despite our romantic nonsense about a 'lone wolf,' a true lone canine finds survival difficult. It is much more vulnerable to attack, starvation, and illness without the coordinated assistance of pack mates.

Each pup learns not only the 'rules' of the pack but also his/her place in the hierarchy, because packs do have a definite 'pecking order.' Every pack has a leader or 'alpha' that may be either male or female, who has earned the respect of the pack. The whole pack defers to the alpha in all things and protects its leader. The alpha eats first, gets the best sleeping spots, gets first choice for mating, and leads the pack when they're on the move or hunting. The alpha makes the final decisions, enforces the rules, sets the pack's routines, and keeps them all safe and fed.

The other pack members fall into groups, depending on their individual natures, but they all follow the alpha. Following the pack leader is completely natural and accepted by canines. Knowing their place in the pack makes them very contented and gives them a great sense of security. They know exactly what's expected of them.

Actually a pack functions very much like a large, successful, and well-run corporation, and that may help you to understand how your pup sees the world. He wants a CEO who's smart, fair, and reasonable, and he wants to understand his place on the corporate ladder. He wants to do good work and be rewarded, but he can't do that in an atmosphere that is confusing, unstable, or stressful. If you've ever suffered working under a boss who was unfair, unclear about expectations, or volatile, you should understand what your pup needs from you.

When that pup enters your life, you have effectively become his or her new pack. While you may supply care, play, and food, many owners neglect to ensure that the dog understands his position in the pack. The resulting insecurity is the main cause of 'behavior problems,' including soiling in the house, because the dog isn't sure who's in charge. If a dog doesn't sense a strong pack leader, he'll feel that he has to take on that role himself, even if he's not ready for it or comfortable with it. After all, somebody has to be in charge, right? Otherwise the pack won't survive.

When you bring home your puppy, you need to step up and become the pack leader that he/she needs, no matter how large or small your pup will be when fully grown. Many people know that they will need to be in charge if they have a large breed dog, but owners of small or toy breeds often don't realize that little dogs need good leadership too. Any dog that is 'pushy,' 'demanding,' 'bossy,' or 'a diva' is a dog trying to fill a perceived lack of leadership in the pack. Unfortunately, these little guys often get away with running their human pack, and this results in the dog doing whatever he wants, including nuisance barking, nipping, jumping up, soiling in the house, etc.

Being the pack alpha is not about dominance, especially physical dominance. That will only inspire fear, not respect, and may result in difficulty with housebreaking and other training. A dog that is more dominant by nature may feel that he has to fight to protect himself if he is frightened. Fear creates uncertainty, not confidence. Pack leaders inspire and build confidence. Alpha is an attitude.

It's also not about physical size, which is good news if you have a large breed dog. Many multi-dog households discover this surprising fact. I remember three very large retrievers who obviously acknowledged an 11-pound Shih Tzu as their alpha. Watching them wait and wiggle with anticipation until she finished eating was quite amusing. Then it was their turn. If they got too pushy, she'd back them off with a stare and a soft growl. Alpha attitude in spades.

So, what do you need to do to fulfill your pup's need for strong leadership? *Consistency* is one of the key factors. Set a routine and stick with it. Walks, potty breaks, meals, play time...all should happen at about the same time every day. Keeping a consistent, repetitive pattern to the day, every day, provides your pup with the feeling that you have everything under control. Knowing what's expected, when, and how to get it makes him or her feel secure and safe in your pack.

Control is another key to being a good alpha. You need to control not only the things that your dog wants, like meals and walks, but also yourself. Alphas don't shout, intimidate, or bully. They just expect to be obeyed. They give commands, not make requests. They speak firmly, not loudly, and they look other dogs right in the eye. They begin and end playtime, and they decide when to give affection and belly rubs. If you doubt that you're in control, your pup will too. If you lose control of yourself and get angry or upset, your pup will feel confused and unsafe. Alphas are always in control!

Alphas also know their pack members and set reasonable expectations. Firm but fair is what's required at all times. If you sleep in four extra hours on Sunday morning, it's not fair to expect that your puppy has been able to hold his bladder that long. It's your bad, not his. Get him outside immediately, praise him when he does his 'business' in the right spot, and clean up the other mess without comment or anger.

Learn his personality so that you can anticipate how he'll react to things. It will help you to set realistic expectations. Is he carefree and laid-back, or is he cautious with new things or in strange situations? Is he everybody's buddy or is he more timid with strangers? Fearless or naturally fearful? Knowing and accepting your pup's personality and character makes you able to adapt routines, training, and management to get the best from him.

Establishing leadership of your pack will make house-training, early behavior training, and everyday living easier for you and your dog(s). Your puppy needs and wants an alpha. You need to step up and take that responsibility. Love him, care for him, and lead him well.

KEN PHILLIPS

Chapter 3: Using Positive Reinforcement

Now that you understand how to be the strong pack leader that your puppy needs, it is time that you learn the importance of positive reinforcement, which you can use during the training process. Training with positive reinforcement is rooted in the old saying 'You can catch more flies with honey than with vinegar.' Your puppy wants to please his alpha, and using that as a training method makes life easier and much more pleasant for both of you.

Positive reinforcement rewards a dog for behaving in the expected manner, but refrains from using loud voices or physical approaches otherwise. There's no real 'punishment' for bad behavior. Punishment is negative reinforcement. If it's not the desired behavior, it's ignored as much as possible. Attention, even negative attention, reinforces bad behavior. Treats, attention, and snuggling can only be achieved by giving the behavior that was desired by the alpha.

Let's take Mario and his puppy, Buddy, as an example.

Mario is an average guy. He adopted Buddy from one of the dog shelters near his neighborhood because he has always wanted a dog to call his own. One day, he decided that Buddy had to be trained. He tried a few methods of training before he settled on one that he felt was right and effective.

First, Mario tried to be the dominant, alpha male in his relationship with Buddy. Whenever Buddy would pull on his leash during walks, Mario would pull him back harder or would smack the side of Buddy's hind legs with his foot. If Buddy chewed on a shoe or a pants leg, Mario would make his disapproval known by forcefully taking the object away and scolding Buddy loudly. This resulted in Buddy being afraid of Mario.

While he did learn not to pull on the leash or chew on anything inappropriate, he also learned that his human companion was scary and could not be trusted completely. Buddy became jumpy and insecure. He would bark at other dogs and would shy away from other people.

When Mario saw how his training method was affecting his dog, he decided to try another way. He trained Buddy with a firm but gentle voice. He never laid a hand on his dog again, except to praise him, or carefully and slowly push or pull him away from a potentially dangerous situation. Mario focused his energy on praising Buddy every time he did something right and correcting him, instead of scolding him, whenever he did something wrong.

The effect on Buddy was immediate. He became eager to please and was no longer afraid of Mario. Buddy learned to enjoy his training sessions, as well as genuinely listen to Mario's commands. The bond between human and dog deepened and both of them became happier.

The story of Mario and Buddy is one that has been repeated again and again in homes where individuals are discovering the wonders and benefits of using positive reinforcement. Instead of punishing dogs because they are committing mistakes they do not fully understand, positive reinforcement asks dog owners worldwide to shift their perspective and focus on the good points of their dog's behavior.

There is a solid scientific basis to why positive reinforcement is very effective as a training method. Dogs are creatures of habit. They value routine and look for patterns in their day-to-day activities. They learn about their companions and environment in the same way a toddler or child does—by repetition.

This means that if a puppy is consistently rewarded for behaving in a certain way, he will continue following that behavioral pattern. Positive reinforcement is a humane and non-threatening way to teach any desired behaviors. It also shows puppies and dogs alike that their human family, and especially their alpha, can be trusted, and that prevents stress and helps them to feel safe.

Confidence, and not fear, is instilled alongside the good habits that form whenever an owner uses positive training methods. Canines are very intelligent and positive reinforcement makes them use that intelligence. They are challenged to figure things out and sometimes you can almost see the wheels turning in their heads. I well remember watching a little American Eskimo pup obviously thinking through the givens of the situation: pee outside, get treat and praise; pee in the kitchen, get ignored. He seemed to reach a conclusion, looked straight at me, and very deliberately started to pee on the kitchen floor. A firm calm 'No' and I whisked him outside, where his peeing in the grass was rewarded. Ears and tail went up and he pranced back inside, very pleased with himself. It was his 'Aha!' moment, and my floors were clean and dry for the next 16 years. He definitely 'Got it!' and was testing his theory.

Positive reinforcement is often paired with negative reinforcement, as in the example above, for speedy results. In the housebreaking situation, it would work like this. If I discover a puddle on the floor, I just clean it up. No words, no recrimination, no dirty looks at the pup, nothing. That behavior has been ignored. However, if I catch him in the act of making a puddle, I react immediately with a firm 'No' and an unhappy face. I grab him and move him as quickly as possible to an acceptable piddle spot. Any peeing there, no matter how little, is lavishly praised with a big smiling face. The pup will naturally prefer the smiling praise to the unhappy 'No'. Wouldn't you? I've reinforced the behavior from both sides and I've made very clear what makes this pack leader happy.

It is important to note that dogs are very good at reading body language, so controlling your physical expressions is important. It's a natural form of communication for them. Dogs use ear and tail position, as well as whole body stance, to let each other know friendliness, challenge, willingness to fight, protectiveness, and pack position. Don't be surprised if your puppy goes belly up—the position of submission—when he meets someone or another dog. He's just acknowledging that they totally outrank him and he accepts it. Make sure that your body language is positive in order to send him the correct messages.

Other desired behaviors can be achieved the same way. If sitting gets a smile and a treat and jumping up doesn't get anything, guess whose butt will start hitting the floor regularly! When you begin house-training, also begin teaching the basic commands, especially 'sit.' Make that pup sit to get a treat, sit to get his meals, and sit before playtime or petting. In a pack, nothing is free; rewards are earned. Be the alpha who demands and rewards acceptable behavior.

Chapter 4: Using Mother Nature to Your Advantage

If you are worried that housebreaking will take a lot of effort and time on your behalf, then fret no more. Puppies, like their adult dog parents, have certain instincts bestowed on them by Mother Nature. Understanding and using these instincts correctly will help make the housebreaking process a lot easier.

In the wild, canines do just about everything, except sleeping and whelping, **outside** their dens.   Mating, socializing, and eating are all non-den activities. This includes elimination. Wolf pups will walk away from the warmth of their littermates and mother in order to relieve themselves. They will make sure that their waste is as far as possible from the pack so that the den won't be discovered by enemies.

In a domestic home, you create that den for your pup by managing and controlling his space. The instinct to move away from the sleeping area for pooping or peeing is something that every dog owner should take advantage of, and it's the basis for easy house-training. This means that you need to manage your pup's space and provide reasonable options to prevent soiling his den. Hopefully, that means that you can pay attention, watch the clock, and get him outside regularly to potty.

At about 10-12 weeks of age, your puppy will hold in his bowel urges for as long as he is capable of, especially if he knows that you will eventually let him out for a potty break. This means that all you have to do is provide him with a place to do his business and give him a routine he can rely on. In time, he will never eliminate in an unacceptable place again.

Remember that a pup's main concern is that his sleeping spot remains unsoiled. He can live with pee or poop in his confinement area, so long as the space he sleeps in is relatively clean. This makes choosing a crate, if you're going to use one, and setting up the 'puppy pen,' or confinement area, very important.

Crates and crate training are often misused and misunderstood. A crate is not a cage or a prison cell for your dog, and it shouldn't be used as one. A crate is a den, your pup's safe sleeping spot. It should be just big enough for him to stand up, turn around, and lay down with his legs stretched out. Too big and he'll have room to soil one end and sleep in the other. Since puppies start small and get bigger, sometimes much bigger, and crates can be somewhat expensive, this can present a bit of a problem.

You can, of course, buy new crates as your pup grows. This works fine for toy dogs that will remain very small even when fully grown. You can have a 'puppy size' and an adult size crate. It's not at all practical, however, for medium to large breed dogs since you could need four (or more) crates to accommodate the pup's growth over his first 18 months of life. There are, thankfully, other solutions.

Most people invest in one good quality crate that will be the right size for their pup when it's grown to adult size. They also purchase a crate divider panel, so they can section off the extra space until it's needed. Effectively, the divider creates a smaller crate inside the bigger one. As the pup grows, you simply move the divider until you don't need it anymore. Some crates come with the divider panel, so look for that. If you don't have a divider panel, you can use a piece or plywood or a sealed up box to block off the excess space.

Proper use of a crate makes not only housebreaking but also all other aspects of raising a pup much easier on both of you. I'll discuss choosing a crate, using it correctly, and helping your pup to feel at home in it in the next chapter.

Puppies, just like dogs, rely on routine. Packs operate under the routine set by their alpha, so following a schedule comes naturally to your puppy. It will take a couple of days, however, for a pup to understand the new schedule you have in mind for him, but once he does, he will rely on it for as long as possible. Puppies naturally follow their internal clock. If their body gets used to peeing and pooping 10-15 minutes right after they eat, then you can expect them to do so until that schedule is replaced by a new one.

If you get your pup from a breeder, they'll be able to tell you what the pup's routine has been. You can then gradually transition that to a schedule that works better for your family and lifestyle. Schedules will also change as the puppy grows because he will have better and better physical control over his elimination needs as he gets older.

Of course, since a pup's urinary tract and digestive system is smaller and works faster than that of an adult dog, you can't expect him to hold his bowel movement for long. However, you can use this internal body clock of his to establish a pattern—something that you can predict, and therefore, incorporate into the routine. Learn his patterns and his signals that he needs to go, and always try to anticipate the need. Proactive is the watchword of housebreaking. Far better too many trips outside than not enough.

Puppies like to return to a previously used spot to eliminate. A pup's waste leaves a distinctive scent that serves as a trigger for the act of eliminating. Once a puppy gets a whiff of his pee on the floor, for example, he will most likely go there to urinate again. This is why you have to rid your floors of any scent that your pup may leave. Disinfect and clean any 'accidents' with effective cleaning solutions like water mixed with white vinegar, or an enzyme-based commercial product such as Nature's Miracle, that will completely remove the odor. Never use a cleaner with ammonia in it—urine contains ammonia! It's as if you didn't clean it at all to a puppy nose. Remember that a canine's sense of smell is thousands of times more sensitive than yours.

If your puppy can only smell his own distinctive elimination scent in his designated soiling area, then he will be all the more encouraged to leave his waste there. This instinct is used in house-training to lure your pup to an acceptable area. You should clean up after him, but the pup will be able to smell where it was. Don't put paper towels that you've used to mop up into your kitchen trashcan because he'll smell them there, and that smell is an instinctive signal for him. Likewise with old towels, cleaning rags, or soiled toys. If you're not washing them immediately, get them out of the house. Don't forget to use some white vinegar in the washer to completely remove the odor.

Keeping the designated soiling spot clean is very important, as is keeping your puppy clean. Although you want him to return to the same area, leaving feces lying around is unhealthy for everyone. Whether it's your own yard or a more public area, always pooper scoop. If you're a city dweller, make the designated spot off the sidewalk, preferably off the curb in the gutter area. Still scoop, please! Un-scooped poopers are not only unsightly and smelly, but they also spread disease and parasitic infestations to other dogs and humans. Scoop the poop wherever it is.

You'll need to keep 'potty smells' off your puppy as well. Being soiled will affect his ability to smell his marked pooper spot. When the smell is actually on *him*, wherever he is smells like his spot, so he'll begin to go anywhere. This is definitely a huge setback to getting him housebroken. Baby wipes work very well for this type of cleanup, but do get the unscented ones. The scented ones are not only very strong for his sensitive sense of smell but can also cause allergic reactions.

Chapter 5: Choosing and Using a Crate

Choosing a Crate

There are many different styles of crates available, but only two are appropriate for puppies: wire or plastic. You will see soft-sided crates and stylish decorative crates that look like furniture. Those are difficult to clean and they are easily destroyed by active puppies during the teething stage. Save those options for when your pup is grown and trained. If they're suitable for your dog, you can invest in one later.

Whether you want a wire or a plastic crate depends on your lifestyle and the general breed of dog that you're getting. Both types have advantages and disadvantages that I'll discuss in detail in a moment but first a word to the budget-minded. Crates, especially for larger breeds, can be rather expensive. However, many people don't use their crates at all once their dog is trained. This means that you can pick up used crates for a lot less at yard sales, on Craigslist, etc. Just make sure it's the size you need and that you disinfect it thoroughly before using it.

Wire crates provide great ventilation and this makes them very popular in hot climates or for dogs with heavy coats. They are also better for dogs that have short muzzles, like the Pekinese, and that may be prone to breathing problems. The air circulation is tremendous in a wire crate. They also don't absorb odors and they have a removable floor tray that pulls out for cleaning. Many of them fold flat (or almost flat) for easy transport and storage. Dividers are easy to use with wire crates, attaching easily and securely, and some models even come with the divider included. Wire crates can come with anywhere from one to three doors, usually on the side, the end, and/or the top, so you need to consider where you'll be placing the crate and where you'll need the door. The door on the top is a great option for a second door, making it easy to pop a young puppy, toy, or treat in and out.

On the other hand, wire crates are not permitted for airline or train travel with your dog. They are also more difficult to move from place to place around your home, for instance moving it from the family room during the day to the bedroom at night. If you have a 'Houdini dog,' wire crates seem to be easier to escape from. And, believe it or not, some dogs manage through contortions to pee and/or poop through the wire sides onto the floor outside the crate. Honestly.

Plastic crates, sometimes referred to as portable 'kennels', may look more confining but they answer many dogs need for a cozy private den. With the carry handle on top and their lighter weight, they are much easier to move around your house. If you plan to travel with your pet, this is the type you will need for the airlines, but make sure that the one you purchase says 'airline approved.' It's not the material or style but rather the construction that needs to meet airline standards, and not all hard plastic crates do. This type of crate comes in different colors, which appeals to many people, and the top half disconnects and can be stacked with the bottom piece for storage. The solid sides make a plastic crate harder for dogs to fuss with the latch and escape from. This type of crate can also be purchased with a door on the top as well as the side/end door.

However, since they are more solid-sided, plastic crates can get rather hot because the air circulation is not as good as in a wire crate. The dog's vision is also limited, which is a plus or a minus depending on your dog's temperament. Some dogs feel very cut off from the rest of the pack in a plastic crate; others do better without the distractions and can calm down more easily. A plastic crate can also be a little more challenging to clean, especially if there's a messy accident. You'll need to remove the top half to have access to the bottom for a thorough cleansing.

Once you've decided which type of crate is right for you, use the size guide below to get the correct-sized crate. Most online pet sites and stores have a lot of information on crate sizing and the sales associates in any pet store can give you great advice as well. Remember that it shouldn't be too big!

Size	Length	Dog's Weight	Example Breeds
Extra Small	24 inches	up to 25 pounds	Yorkie, Chihuahua, Pug
Small	30 inches	25-40 pounds	Scottie, Mini Poodle, Sheltie
Medium	36 inches	40-70 pounds	Beagle, Bulldog, Cocker Spaniel

Large	42 inches	70-90 pounds	Border Collie, Labrador, Golden Retriever
Extra Large	48 inches	90-110 pounds	Collie, Husky, German Shepherd
Giant	54 inches	over 110 pounds	Great Dane, Saint Bernard, Newfoundland

Introducing the Crate

The quickest way to make your puppy HATE his crate is to force him into it! Any pup needs a little time to investigate the crate and decide it's a good place, not a scary one. Make it cozy for him with a crate mat, old blanket or beach towel, or something else comfy on the floor. Don't waste money at this point on a fancy little bed or a memory foam mat. It'll just get chewed up or messed on. Once housebreaking and teething are behind you both, you can invest in nicer bedding. At that time you can even put a bolster-sided bed inside the crate.

Assemble and put the crate in its place *when your puppy can't see you do it.* The process can be intimidating for him. All the banging, big pieces, and movement can make the crate a scary thing right from the start. If it makes the pack leader flustered, angry, or say bad words...it's definitely not a good thing! So surprise him with it, like a kid's first bike on Christmas morning. Your objective is to let the pup discover it, explore it, and enter it on his own terms. Prop the door open, put some treats inside the crate, and let him check it out. Sit near it and put some treats in front of the crate to lure him over. Then toss a few inside. Let the pup get comfortable with entering and leaving the crate on his own.

When he seems OK with it, swing the door shut behind him when he goes in. Don't latch it; just quietly push it closed. When he turns around to sniff the door, open it up for him. Gradually leave it closed for longer and longer. (Lots of praise goes along with this process). Eventually give him something that will keep him occupied for a little bit, close the door, and move away from the crate but keep an eye on him.

A sleeping pup can be transferred into a crate with the door left open. When he wakes up, he'll be in his own little den, but not shut in. Again let him explore, move in and out, and decide it's a good thing. You want him to accept his crate as a safe place where good things, like special treats, happen. His instinct is to have a den so, as long as the crate is 'good' in his eyes, he'll settle in and may even curl up to nap in there on his own.

During the day, the crate should be in a communal area or in his confinement area, if you're not home. Dogs are social and he needs to keep up with what's happening in his pack. He'll watch and learn. At night, it should be in or very near your bedroom. Generally speaking, a dog should not wear a collar when he's crated. It can easily get snagged and cause serious injury to your pup. Leave the collar, with the leash attached, where you can grab it quickly on your way outside, or you can use a slip lead.

If you have children, keep them out of his space! A pup needs a place to escape distractions, such as active children, from time to time and to find a little peace in his own snug den. Children need to learn to respect his right to do that.

Chapter 6: What You'll Need

You've got a puppy and a crate, so now what? There are a few other items you'll need in order to start housebreaking effectively. Gather them before you try to start, and you'll be ready to go.

Get a good enzyme-based cleaner, such as Nature's Miracle, or stock in a good supply of white vinegar [mix about 50-50 with water to use]. You need these to neutralize potty smells so the pup doesn't re-use the spot. He can smell many many things that you can't, and his 'cleaned up' bathroom spots are one of them. You'll also need them to clean any soiled bedding or toys. Keeping some in a spray bottle for quick-wiping floors or crates is helpful, too. Along with the cleaning solution, you'll need some rags or old towels for wiping up. Paper towels get way too expensive and are harder to use, especially if you need to wipe the puppy.

Another handy item is called a slip lead. It's a type of leash with a big loop that slips over the dog's head quickly. Once on, the loop tightens to neck size. Vet offices use these because they're very quick and easy to get on and off, and they're also used in dog shows. The advantage in using one when you're housebreaking is that you may need to scoop up puppy and get him out right away. You can put on the slip lead while you're headed out the door without having to snap on or buckle a collar. A crated dog should not have a collar on when he's in the crate (it can get caught and seriously injure your pup), so a slip lead is faster and easier than messing with getting a collar on and attaching the leash, especially for middle of the night trips. Slip leads are also used in other training, so it's worth having one around.

If you're going to use paper training, you need to get a good supply of those as well. Many people no longer get a physical daily paper, so newspapers can be hard to come by nowadays. If you don't have newspaper, go to anyplace that sells moving supplies. The paper they sell by the box for wrapping articles when packing to move is just unprinted newspaper in big sheets. If you know anyone who's moved recently, they probably have part of a box left over that they'll gladly give you.

'Wee wee' pads, or piddle pads, are a slightly more expensive option, but they have certain advantages over paper. They resemble thin diapers, and they are scented to attract your puppy to potty on them. Also like diapers, they absorb liquid so you won't have rivulets of pee escaping onto the floor as often as you might with paper. If you go this route, don't buy the holding trays they sell for the pads at this point in time. Many puppies find them 'scary' and they won't use the pad if it's in the tray.

Although pads cost more than newspaper, they can be a really good choice, particularly for toy or smaller dogs. Many apartment dwellers, especially in cities, use the pads for the life of the dog. Once a dog is used to using them, pee pads can provide an acceptable indoor soiling spot if you need to be away from home for longer than usual. They're also handy for dogs recovering from illnesses or surgery, elderly dogs who have developed trouble 'holding it', or in cases of horribly inclement weather.

'Litter pan' training is another increasingly popular choice in both cities and in condos or apartments anywhere. This is usually used for smaller dogs, generally those weighing 10 pounds or less, but there are ways to adapt it for larger dogs if you have the space. There are several types available, and some can be placed out on an enclosed patio or secure balcony. Most use pellets or fake grass, but you can actually get patches of live turf delivered monthly for this purpose also. If this sounds workable for your situation, do some research and pick out your system. You'll want to train your puppy to use it right from the start.

The other thing you'll need is a baby gate or two, and again you may be able to pick some up at yard sales or rescue them from a friend's attic. Make sure that the barrier material is close together enough that little paws can't get caught in it! You will need to 'pen' your pooch while you're away. A puppy can be crated for only so long. Then he's going to have to go and he's going to need to move around. Baby gates can close off an area such as a small bathroom or laundry room, so that the pup can sleep in his crate and still have access to a papered area for elimination. Otherwise, you're forcing him to soil his den, and that's not fair. Good alphas are always fair and reasonable, so be prepared to create a managed puppy space.

The other puppy things such as collars, bowls, and toys are the fun stuff you've already started collecting. Don't go too overboard with these because they'll need to be replaced with more appropriate sizes as your puppy grows. A final word about 'treats,' however, is in order. I've already talked about treats and you'll hear more about using them for training in later chapters. But what do I mean by 'treats?' The treats you'll use are called 'training treats.' These are very tiny little bits of yummy stuff, about the size of a pea, which dogs love. Because they're so small, you can feed them often as rewards without overfeeding your pup. Keep them by the door so you can grab them on your way out to reward a successful potty trip. There are also little bags for them that can clip onto your clothes so you'll always have them with you to reward good puppy behavior. If you're home all day with the pup, the treat bags are really handy. Training your pup is about 'reward the act, not after the fact.'

Now you have the things that you need for fast effective house-training, you just need to understand the methods outlined in the next chapter. Successful housebreaking depends upon YOU, alpha dog, not your puppy! So now it's time to do your homework.

Chapter 7: Methods of Housebreaking

There are two main ways to housebreak your new puppy: paper training and crate training. Crate training is one of the quickest ways to housebreak your pup but not the best method if you must leave your pup for a longer period of time than your pup is able to hold it. For people who must work all day or be away for long periods of time, I recommend a combination of both methods.

Paper Training

The paper-training method is where you use newspapers and encourage your puppy to use these for going to the bathroom. You can also use special 'wee wee' pads that are scented with a chemical that attracts the puppy to use them. You can get these at any local pet store. They can make training easier but they can be more costly as well. If you intend to continue using the pads, make sure you start with them and not paper. Don't mix newspaper and pads or your results will be very inconsistent.

The first thing you want to do is choose a confinement area, either in a very small room or a room that you can enclose with baby gates. Most people choose a bathroom, laundry room or kitchen area because these rooms are usually covered in tile or other flooring that is easy to keep clean. The confinement area should only be big enough for your pup's bed, food and water bowls, and his designated potty area.

There should be no visible floor space in the confinement area. The floor should have the bed or crate in one section, and newspapers or pads should cover the rest of the space. By using a small area, you are encouraging your pup to use the covered area of the floor to relieve himself. This will get him used to doing his business on the newspapers or pads. He won't potty in his bed or where he eats for reasons we have already discussed, and since it's the only other space available, the potty area becomes a natural choice. The instincts that Mother Nature gave him will guide him away from his 'den' area to eliminate.

When he does soil on the newspapers, try to clean them up as quickly as possible. You may want to consider leaving a rag that has a little of his urine on it in the designated spot to help him recognize where he's suppose to go, if you're using newspaper. The pads are already scented to attract the puppy to go there. There are also house-training sprays you can buy at any big pet store that serve the same purpose. The pheromones in them attract puppy back to the right spot. These sprays can also be used outdoors if you want to direct him to a certain area.

Once your pup becomes accustomed to pottying on the newspapers, you can make the covered area smaller. You should have noticed which section of the area he has used most often, and keep all that section well covered. Start uncovering the area very close to his crate/bed and bowls. The goal is to continuously limit the designated 'inside potty area' by making the papered area smaller and smaller at the same time giving him frequent access to his 'outdoor potty area'. Therefore it's important that you spend as much time as possible with your puppy so you can get him to his outdoor area as often as possible.

The key to quick and successful housebreaking when using the paper training method really depends on how much supervised training you spend with your pup. The more times you can get him outside to do his business and reward him, the quicker he will learn.

Crate Training

The second method of housebreaking involves the use of a crate. You want to make sure the crate isn't too large—it should be just big enough to fit a sprawled sleeping puppy. As discussed earlier, dogs do not like to urinate or defecate in their sleeping areas or dens. Once pups are safely mobile, their mothers push them outside so they can go potty.

Crate training helps puppies learn how to control their bladder and bowels. Ideally you should take a puppy outside about every hour to start. Gradually lengthen the time between trips, within the limitations of his little bladder (see next chapter). It's important that you keep your eye on the clock. You don't want to lose track of the time and force your puppy to go in his crate. The more he can feel positive that you'll let him out to relieve himself in a timely fashion, the more incentive he has to wait for you. He wants praise from his pack leader, but he also needs to feel that he can trust you and rely on you.

When your puppy is not crated, watch carefully for signs that he needs to go out. Most dogs have a 'pre-potty' ritual of sniffing, circling, whining, etc., that he'll use to try to let you know what he needs. With a little observation, and a few accidents, you'll learn your dog's potty signals. Once that starts, pick him up and get him outside or onto paper (or a piddle pad) right away. You also need to understand that he can stop his urine, but once he starts a poop, leave him be. He can't control it and, if you try to move him to a better spot, you'll have a trail to clean up instead of a pile.

There are certain times that all puppies need to go out, so learn these times and avoid accidents.

- Immediately after waking up, in the morning or from a nap
- After any excitement or play
- Within 10-30 minutes of eating
- After a big drink of water
- The absolute last thing before bed at night

Carry the puppy outside to prevent accidents between the crate, or wherever you are, and the doorway. Some pups anticipate a bit too much and they'll go right in front of the door, seconds away from being in the correct spot. So provide 'taxi service' for a little one. Also, unless they're truly desperate (or scared), most puppies won't pee on you. After all, you're Mom and Alpha rolled into one!

Whenever the puppy is inside the home, but cannot be directly supervised, he should be placed in his crate. A good time would be when you're cooking, watching TV, taking a shower or even away from the house for a short period. Take your pup out right before crating him, and again as soon as you let him out of the crate.

Another way to keep your puppy supervised but still be able to do things is to use 'tethering'. Basically you attach him to you via his leash, so he goes where you go. This gives you the freedom to get some housework done. Alternatively, you can tether him to something like a table leg if you're going to be staying in one room of your home, for example, cooking. You need to keep a close eye on him still, and be prepared to drop what you're doing if he shows signs of thinking about going potty. Tethering does, however, give him time outside the crate to stretch, investigate, and learn. It's a great option when you're on the patio or deck, or if you're in the yard. Never let the pup roam unsupervised in the yard, even if it's securely enclosed. They will try to eat anything! I had one little guy who devoured a squished frog, bones and all, before I could stop him, and another who insisted on trying to eat acorns. Needless to say, both experienced severe 'gastric distress.' You also should know that many decorative plants are toxic to dogs.

You definitely want to crate your puppy at bedtime. Sleeping alone is probably a new experience for him, and a slightly scary one. Puppies generally sleep in a pile, the whole litter snuggled close together with their mother. You can ease the transition for your pup by giving him a stuffed toy to curl up with as a fake littermate and, if he's very young, a well-wrapped hot water bottle under the bedding. The ticking of a clock placed nearby can help to mimic the sound of Mom's heartbeat and it reassures many pups. Also, putting a piece of clothing that you've worn into the crate with him can calm his fears since he can cuddle up to your smell. A little consideration for his sudden sense of isolation at night can make it much easier for both of you to get some sleep!

Expect your puppy to have to go potty in the middle of the night for a while, so put his crate in or very near your bedroom if at all possible. He's still a baby after all. It's a good idea if you are proactive about getting him out by setting an alarm clock. Keep whatever shoes, coat, keys, etc., that you'll need when taking him out laid out ready to grab and go for those middle of the night jaunts. Have his leash pre-attached to his collar, so you can just snap the collar on him, or use a slip lead. These trips will only be necessary until he's 5-6 months old. As he gets older, he'll sleep longer, have more control over his bladder, and begin to wake you if he really needs to go. Within a few months, he'll be sleeping through the night without a problem.

The ultimate goal of crate training is to never let your pup go potty in the house. This requires that you (or someone) be there to take him out on time, so you need to fit that into your schedule without fail. If you must be gone more than five hours, use the paper-training method while you are away and set up a managed confinement area with his crate in it.

When done right, there are many advantages to crate training. Crate training can effectively teach a puppy that when the urge to go pee or poop occurs, they are capable of holding it (within their limitations of course). It fits wonderfully with their natural instincts as well. Crate training also strengthens the alpha-pack bond that you are building with your puppy. He is learning that he can rely on you to see to his needs; therefore, he feels he can trust you and have respect for his pack leader. This is the main reason why puppy owners who use crate training have found it to be a quicker way of not only housebreaking their pup, but also teaching other desirable behaviors.

Litter Pan Training

As mentioned earlier, litter pan training is growing in popularity. Many dogs take to it very well, and it provides an easier cleaner indoor option than just a space on the kitchen floor. For dog owners living in high-rise buildings, people with limited mobility, or dogs who are unsuited for the weather where they live, pan training allows ease and comfort for both owners and dogs. A dog trained to a litter pan will still potty outdoors when going 'walkies,' but he has another option as well. Since little dogs need to go more often than their bigger cousins, it's very helpful for them to have an acceptable indoor area where they can relieve themselves while their owners are away from home. Eight hours for a large dog is like 'holding it' for 24 hours to a little guy! Not a very reasonable expectation.

If a litter pan of some type is your chosen route, make sure you have it ready to go before beginning house-training. Find a convenient spot in your home to place it, and don't move it around except when you need to set up a confinement area. Your puppy needs to learn where to find it. You can relocate it once he's trained.

If your dog is not a toy breed, you'll need to provide a larger pan as he grows. Many people start with a traditional dog litter pan and change to a round one, since dogs like to circle before pooping. For a larger dog, this could even be something like a 'kiddie pool', perhaps moved into the garage or basement after he's trained.

Make sure that your dog can easily enter the pan without climbing or jumping. It needs to be simple for him to get in and out! You may need to cut the entryway down a bit lower so that he can step in. Some people like the pellets that are sold as litter, and there are several different types, and others just use a piddle pad in the pan. If your pup doesn't seem to like it, or tries to eat it, change to a different type of absorbing medium. [Cat litter doesn't work very well for most dogs because it really gets stuck in their feet.] The fake grass models have a tray underneath which collects the urine, but many folks like to line that with wee wee pads for quicker, easier cleaning.

Be aware, if you're not already, that although young male pups squat, as he matures he'll lift his leg to urinate. By that time you need to make provisions so that he doesn't pee over the top of the pan or onto the wall. You can purchase posts or little plastic fire hydrants, scented with attractant, to give him something to aim at, or use a pan with higher sides. If you have multiple dogs, you may need multiple pans. They sometimes don't want to share and won't use a pan that's already been soiled.

To train your pup to a litter pan, *follow the same procedures as crate training.* You just take the pup to the litter pan instead of taking him outside to the yard. If you need to be away for a while, set up a confinement area with the litter pan inside, just as you would do with paper training. Be sure to cover the rest of the floor with paper (in case of accidents) until your pooch is reliable with the pan.

Just as with newspaper, pads, and even the yard, the litter pan should be kept as clean as possible. Clean up messes as soon as possible, and change the litter following the instructions that come with it. Empty the pan for a thorough cleansing with disinfectant cleaner at least once a week, and hose off the plastic turf as well.

Crazy Training Plan

If you would like to streamline the housebreaking process, and you can completely free yourself from any other responsibilities, work or family, for a couple of days, then this 'extreme' method might be just the thing for you. It's very effective and creates a strong bond, but it does take its toll on you. If you're not a little bit crazy and open to things that are 'outside the box,' skip to the next chapter now. If, like me, you're a bit of a risk-taker, read on.

The 'crazy' way to house-train your pup, within his physical bladder limits of course, is to be *completely proactive*. The pup never goes on the floor, not once. How do you achieve this miracle, you ask? With self-sacrifice and a total focus on the task, allowing no distractions. It's just you, puppy, and housebreaking.

This will work with a litter pan or a pad as well as going outdoors. It's actually a simple procedure, a sort of 'extreme crate training,' but you have to 'suck it up' and follow through—that's the craziness. It's 24/7 on your part until you reach his physical limits. After that, you never ask him to exceed those limits.

Still with me? Then here's how it goes. You bring puppy home and let him potty before you bring him inside. Ten minutes later, you take him out again (or take him to the pan or pad). Praise a successful trip! If he doesn't go, give him another ten minutes and then out again. After each successful potty break, you add five minutes to the time between trips, so you'd wait 15 minutes and then go out again. After each unsuccessful trip, repeat the same interval.

You need to continue this all day and all night, following and adjusting the schedule. Wake up (use an alarm), wake him up (really), and go out. (I slept on the sofa by the door to facilitate the process, while puppy slept tethered on the floor next to me.) Work some playtime in between some of the trips, and don't forget to wedge in some food for both you and the pup. Watch some TV together. But keep track of the time! You'll become a little zombie-like, but that's OK. Think of it as a short-term extreme sporting event. Stay focused on your mission!

A three-month-old pup will settle into a 3-4 hour maximum interval between trips. Once you know what that limit is for your pup, you can make arrangements to let him relieve himself within that interval. You can also crate him and crawl into bed until your next puppy potty break (set the alarm).

Although you'll need about a day to fully recover, depending on what time of day you brought him home and started the process, you'll also have a very accurate idea of his bathroom habits and needs. You will have learned his potty rituals—does he sniff or circle, or both? (This can help you prevent future 'accidents' if he needs to go earlier than usual for some reason.) You've earned his trust, and he can count on you to meet, even anticipate, his needs. He's never eliminated anywhere except where you, his pack leader, have approved, so he won't be inclined to start. Even young as he is, he'll come to you for a potty break. And, in spite of the sleep disruption, it is time spent working together that can give you a very strong bond with your dog. Packs work cooperatively for the good of all, and that's what you two have just done together!

The follow-up is simply assuring that you never expect

him, or force him, to exceed his capabilities. You get him to his designated area within his time limit, period. If you can't be there to do it, then you find someone who can help you out. This means at night, too. Set the alarm, take him for his potty break, praise, and go back to bed. Once he's 6 months old or so and has full control of himself, he'll be *extremely* reliable (and sleeping through the night).

Chapter 8: Creating a Schedule For Puppies

Understanding Bladder Limitations

The younger your puppy is, the greater his limitation when it comes to the time he can control his bladder. The younger dogs are, the less control they have over their sphincter muscles, hence, the more frequently they will need to urinate. In young pups, there's no lag time between urge and elimination, and they lack the muscle control to 'hold it.'

A frequently used formula for estimating the number of hours for which a puppy can hold its bladder is N+1, where N equals puppy's age in months. For example, if your puppy is 2 months old, he should be able to hold his bladder for approximately 3 hours <u>at most</u>. Many people, however, simplify this to 'age in months equals time in hours'. So two hours would be reasonable and comfortable for a 2-month-old puppy.

In instances with crate training especially, if your puppy is 3 months old and we use the puppy bladder formula, he should be able to hold his urine for 3 to 4 hours tops, so keeping your puppy crated for longer than 4 hours is way too much to ask of him. *Also remember, smaller breeds have smaller bladders and will have to go sooner and more often.*

If you wait too long and force your pup to mess his crate, you are only creating more problems for yourself down the road. This creates potential problems with him being stuck inside the crate and having to sleep in his mess, and it interferes with his natural instinct to keep his den clean. You'll have a frustrated and filthy puppy to clean up! For this reason, we do not recommend confining your puppy to a crate if you must leave him longer then he is capable of holding his bladder. Make sure he has a secure confinement area, such as is used in paper training.

By six months of age, you no longer need to use the puppy bladder formula because from here on out your dog will most likely be able to hold his bladder for up to nine hours (although over 8 hours should only be asked of him in rare instances).

This is the maximum even for adult dogs—he'll feel urgency before that, so you shouldn't make your pet companion wait nine hours just because he should be able to. Always make arrangements to have a friend or a neighbor let him out when you cannot be there in a timely fashion for him to relieve himself.

Sample Schedule for a 3-month-old Puppy

Based on the above formula for a 3-month-old puppy, we calculate that he can hold his bladder for up to 4 hours maximum.

The very first thing you must do when you get up in the morning is to immediately take your puppy outside to his designated area. (This means no brushing teeth or putting the coffee on, alpha dog—your puppy comes first!). Always use the same words as a verbal cue that the pup will come to associate with elimination. To this day I still tell my dogs to hurry up and 'go pee pee,' and they know exactly what I mean. The actual words don't matter as long as you're consistent with using them; it's a simple association of sounds with actions. 'Rumplestiltskin' works as well as 'go pee pee,' so suit yourself. I've heard everything from 'do your duty,' 'time for business,' and 'bombs away'. Choose a cue phrase you can live with and use it consistently.

If you want to train him to use bells to let you know when he needs out, now is the time to start to use that sound regularly as a cue as well. Hang the bells by the door and touch them every time you take the pup out. Your puppy will learn to associate the sound of the bells with going out to relieve himself. As he grows up, he'll learn to ring the bells by himself to alert you to his needs. This is a popular option, and it sure beats having your dog scratch at the door.

It's important to give him time to sniff around. Sniffing will allow him to find his previous potty spot and reinforce the new habit. When he goes, give him so much lavish praise that he feels like he's SUPER pup. Then bring him back inside and allow him to have some supervised playtime. NEVER let him run freely through the house without supervision or you're asking for accidents. This is important. If you want to make the coffee or start breakfast, use the tethering technique to give him some roam time under supervision or put up the baby gates.

Let's assume your pup makes his first elimination at 9:00 a.m. in the morning, then according to the figure we calculated for his age, 1:00 p.m. is the *latest* he should be taken out for his bathroom run. If possible try to make it a bit sooner. The other times for the pup to be taken out would be 4:00 p.m., 8:00 p.m., and then 12:00 a.m., since you're obviously a late riser. It's important to keep the same schedule daily, even on the weekends. Consistency is also a key to success.

At 3 months of age, your pup won' t be able to make it through an entire night without a quick potty trip. Remember, your pup is just a baby, so you will need to set your alarm at night around 3-4 am for a quick trip outside. If he's sleeping, take him out anyway. Keep a coat and shoes handy, carry the puppy, and get outside. (I know this is totally obnoxious in the winter, but it's necessary for a short while.) Praise without getting him too excited, return him to the crate, and fall back into your bed.

Your pup will also need to be taken out 10 to 30 minutes after each meal. All dogs are different so make a mental note of how long your pup takes after a meal before he has to go. Other crucial times to take your pup out are after a nap or after time spent in vigorous play or chewing on chew toys. The more vigilant you are with paying attention to such events, the faster your pup will become housebroken.

SCHEDULE #1 [When the Owner is Home]
3-Month-old Puppy

8 am Wake up. **Immediately** take pup out.

8:10-8:30 am Supervised roam time while alpha is drinking coffee.

8:30 am Food and water.

8:45 am Take Out.

9:00 am Supervised roam time.

9:30 am Take Out – then confine.

1:00 pm Take Out – then food and water.

1:15 PM Go Out.

1:30 PM Free Period in Kitchen or Supervised.

2:00 PM Take Out – then Confine.

6:00 pm Take Out – then food and water.

6:15 pm Take Out.

7:15 pm Take Out – then Confine.

9:00 pm Take Out – then give last water for the day.

9:15 pm Take Out.

9:30 pm Supervised roam time.

10:00 pm Take Out – then Confine.

11:30-12:00 am Take Out – Confine for overnight.

*If the above schedule was followed for one week and the puppy was over 3 months or older, your puppy should be completely 95% house broken in a week or so, with only the occasional accident. As your puppy gets older and can go longer periods without an accident, adjust the above schedule accordingly.

SCHEDULE #2 [When the Owner Works]
3-Month-old Puppy

6:00 am Wake up. **Immediately** take pup out.

6:10-6:30 am Supervised roam time.

6:45 am Food and water.

7:00 am Take Out – Confine when owner leaves for day (leave safe chew toy to keep puppy entertained).

11:00am Make arrangements for someone to let pup out if possible.

11:15 Food & Water.

11:30 Take Out and Confine.

3:30 pm Make arrangements for someone to let pup out if possible.

5:30 pm Take Out.

5:45 Supervised roam time

6:00 pm Confine. (Your time!)

7:30 pm Take Out – Supervised roam time with family.

8:00 pm Small meal or snack and water (remove water afterwards)

8:30 pm Take Out – Supervised roam time with family.

9:00 pm Take Out – More roam time or confine.

11:00 pm Take Out – Confine for overnight.

NOTE: If you are unable to make arrangements for someone to take your pup out while you are working, then <u>do not confine him to a crate</u> for that period. Set up a confined area for him as explained under paper training. This schedule is a sample idea only; adjust the times to what works best for you. But once you have made up your own schedule, stick to it!

As your dog gets older and can hold his bladder longer, you can increase his roam times and decrease how often he needs to go out. Supervise him when he's loose to minimize random 'accidents.'

Chapter 9: Do's and Don'ts of House Training

Basic House Training Do's

1. **DO** remember: 'Any doubt, take him out!' Too often is much better than too infrequently.

2. **DO** give your pup consistent verbal potty cues such as 'want to go out?" before you take him outdoors and "go pee pee" once he is outside.

3. **DO** praise your puppy lavishly when he makes potty in his outdoor designated area. If he does it right, let him know!

4. **DO** make a potty schedule and stick to it. Consistency is the key and will expedite the process and make your puppy a better-adjusted pet.

5. **DO** confine your puppy in a crate, part of the kitchen, or makeshift "den" certain periods of the day and for the night. It is the best way for him and for you to teach him control of his body functions.

6. **DO** take your puppy to his toilet area:

- First thing every morning
- After every meal and drink of water
- After every nap
- After every play period or excitement
- Right before bedtime
- Whenever taking him in and out of his cage

7. **DO** pay attention to whining, sniffing floor, or walking in circles and promptly TAKE OUT! A good alpha knows his pack, so learn to read his signals.

8. **DO** clean up with NATURE'S MIRACLE or white vinegar to get rid of odors so your puppy won't be tempted to go there again. Don't forget to use some when you wash clean up rags or any soiled clothing, bedding, or toys as well.

9. **DO** feed your puppy a nutritious diet on a consistent schedule and he will begin to eliminate on a consistent schedule. Canned food will cause looser stools, so feed mainly kibble and no table scraps.

Basic House Training Don'ts

1. **DO NOT** rub your pup's nose in his accidents. Your puppy doesn't understand why you're doing that nasty thing! Nobody made a fuss before, and the pup will not relate the punishment, regardless of its form, together with something he has done without incident numerous times before, especially if he did it more than 60 seconds ago. Dogs live in the NOW. This housebreaking method is cruel and unsuccessful, and it does great damage to the trust bond between a pup and his pack leader.

2. **DO NOT** punish your pup if you don't catch him in the act. He will not understand the connection. Good pack leaders are fair, so don't go overboard because you've had a bad day. He doesn't understand that either. 'Not caught in the act, then don't react.'

3. **DO NOT** yell at your pup if you do catch him in the act. Quickly, but calmly, pick him up and without raising your voice firmly say "No." Carry him outside. It may help to push his tail down while you are carrying him, as it will help stop him from peeing until you get him outside. Praise the outside pee, even if it's just a few drops! The desired behavior is ALWAYS rewarded.

4. **DO NOT** give feed your puppy extra food, except tiny earned training treats, while you are house training. It will make it too difficult to establish a digestive routine. You want to be able to predict when he'll need to go, so you can get him outside beforehand.

5. **DO NOT** expect your pup to hold it longer than what can be expected for his age. Instead create a confinement area to accommodate his need for an indoor potty area if you need to be away longer than is reasonable. Bladder size is basic biology, and good pack leaders are fair. Don't set him up for failure!

6. **DO NOT** allow your pup the unsupervised run of the house. Apart from other dangers, you can't housebreak him if he's not in sight. You need to know if and when there's an accident for both cleanup and for schedule adjustment.

Housebreaking Rules for the Entire Family

The list below is just a sample of house rules that you can use during the housebreaking process. Feel free to add, subtract or modify the rules as you see fit. However, be sure that all of your family members are made aware of the rules.

Remember that consistency is important to a pup. If he is corrected by you every time he pees anywhere but his soiling area, and then not corrected by someone else, your pup will only get confused. A pack functions as a unit, so make sure your whole family is on the same page for the benefit of your new pet. Housebreaking, and all other training, will become a long and frustrating process if you don't work together. Communicate the rules with your family, and make sure they all agree to it.

HOUSE RULES

1. The puppy is a member of the family. He should be treated with respect and kindness. His den is his private space.

2. The puppy is only allowed to pee or poop in his soiling area or outside the house.

3. It is everyone's responsibility to clean up after the puppy right away.

4. Everyone should participate in the training and housebreaking of the puppy.

5. Everyone needs to use the same "cue" words to encourage your puppy to go potty.

6. Everyone should follow the list of the puppy's scheduled potty times.

7. Do not let the pup sleep or climb onto the bed or couch until he is reliably potty trained.

8. The pup's schedule needs to be followed all the time.

You can write the agreed-upon House Rules and place it where everyone can see it. You can also post the pup's schedule next to the House Rules in order to help everyone remember his responsibilities.

Chapter 10: The 7 Days of Housebreaking

Day 1: Pay Attention & Know Your Pack!

If you've just brought your pup home from his breeder's house, then there is a large chance that he will want to pee and poop. He will be nervous, so before you bring him in your home, allow him to walk around a bit in a safe area outside so he can do his business.

On the very first day of your pup's housebreaking, the one thing you should keep in mind is this: pay attention. At this point in the process, you won't have a clear- cut idea of how long it will take for him to pee and poop after eating, or between naps. Stay with him for as long as possible. Get to know your pup as you would a child of your own.

Is he friendly or shy? How does he approach new things? Is he curious, or does he hold back? How often does he go to his bowl for a drink?

After your pup goes potty, give your pup a chance to check out the house. This is best done with your pup off leash, but follow and watch out for potty accidents. Let him roam the house as he pleases. Show him where his soiling area is and where his crate is. Tell your family members beforehand not to crowd the pup or scare him with loud sounds. Let him have some time and space to come to terms with his new surroundings.

Remember, this is all new to him. Let him ease into your family. Instead of having the kids or your family members rush over to pet him, allow the puppy to come to each of you when he is ready. Be smaller, by sitting or kneeling, so you're not a huge thing looming over him. This is a crucial part of his upbringing, as this stage will determine how he interacts with the people in his new home. Don't rush it.

When it is time for your puppy's meal, make sure you feed him in the designated puppy area. Take him for a potty break very soon afterwards.

In addition, you should also watch out for the same cues while playing with your pup. Some pups, out of sheer excitement, tend to pee all of a sudden. Be alert. If your pup squats in the middle of playtime and you don't think you can pick him up, don't panic and yell at him. Gently tell him no and take him outside.

By the end of the first day, you should have a good idea of your pup's elimination schedule. Your pup should have also peed or pooped in his soiling area at least once.

Day 2-4: Follow a Strict Schedule, Be Consistent

On days two to four of the housebreaking process, you should establish both the rules and your pup's potty schedule. The sooner you start following it, the quicker your pup will become housebroken.

Remember to take your pup outside immediately after his meals and ask the question, "Do you want to go OUT?" This will become a verbal cue for the future. Don't allow him back in until he does his duty. He may get a bit distracted but chances are, it won't take long. Whenever he potties outside, praise him lavishly. That is the key to success. Puppies love to please.

Once he's done, it's ok to let your puppy roam around the house again, or take him for a walk. Establish that it's potty first, then 'walkies.' If you don't, he'll learn to 'hold it' as long as he can in order to get a longer walk! Too many owners inadvertently teach their dogs this. They'll end the walk as soon as puppy's business is taken care of. Walks should be a pre-established length so they continue after the potty break. That way, your dog won't postpone going just to get a nice walk.

Don't forget to remove his water bowl before going to bed and to set your alarm for the middle of the night bathroom run, especially if you are crating your pup.

Day 5-6: Continue to Practice the Cue Words

Aside from "no" and "sit," your puppy should be introduced to cue words like, "go pee-pee" or "go poopie" and to any sound cues like bells.

By this time, your pup should be familiar with his designated soiling areas. He should know that he is expected to eliminate in a certain place only. There might have been accidents during the past days, but your pup should show marked improvement in using the soiling area and in following the house rules.

By this time your pup should also have a schedule that is clear to both of you. For example, he should know that he can rely on you to let him out of his crate every hour or every two hours in order to pee or poop.

At this point in the housebreaking process, he is associating your command words with the praise you've been giving him. Practice positive reinforcement by rewarding your puppy for following your commands.

You can also begin using hand signals for your pup to follow. For example, whenever your puppy goes to the soiling area to pee or poop, exaggerate the motion of pointing at the floor and say your cue word(s) in a firm voice.

After a few well-timed signals from you, your pup will know that when you move your hand in a certain pattern, or when you repeat a familiar (hopefully smiley!) face, you are asking him to do something specific or are pleased with what he's done.

Day 7: Put It All Together

Finally, it is time to put your pup to the test. Dedicate as much time on this day as you can to spend with him. As soon as he wakes up, open his crate, and instead of carrying him or leading him to his soiling area on a leash, have him follow you over to his soiling area and give the command and signal for him to do his business.

Go over all of the rules and commands during the day. Think of this as a final examination. Your puppy should be used to following his schedule with you. He should no longer pee or poop inside his crate.

Accidents outside his crate or designated areas should be few and far in between. He should demonstrate enough initiative to visit his soiling area on his own, even if you don't ask him to. Be ecstatic if he uses the bells or comes to you to be taken out!

Your puppy should also be aware of what your command words mean. Remember to reward him generously every time he does something right, and to correct him gently if he does something wrong. Never use his crate as a punishment! Try to anticipate potential bad behavior and redirect him into more acceptable activities.

Seven days of constant practice and training might seem a short time to have a fully housebroken pup, but if you did everything with patience and understanding, then there is no doubt that your puppy will have learned the essential rules of living in your pack, alpha dog!

If Accidents Do Happen...

Don't panic if your puppy has an occasional accident. Just because your 5-month-old puppy has an occasional accident in the house is no reason to think he's not "getting it." Young puppies still don't have full control over their bladders and bowels yet.

Remember your little guy will generally gain better control over his system at about 6+ months of age or so. Some will gain this control earlier or later, it all depends on the individual dog and how much you were able to supervise his training. Puppies at this age should not be punished for accidents nor will it help to speed the housebreaking process in any way.

The best tools an owner can have when housetraining are patience and consistency. Following an established set of rules will help avoid confusion, which goes a long, long way for the puppy. He needs clear leadership and direction to be successful. Hopefully by now you have begun implementing the information in this book and realize that training your dog or puppy is a pretty simple task if you stay alert and stick to your schedule.

Just make sure to remember the three rules to success:

- **Stay consistent.**
- **Stay positive.**
- **Stay patient.**

With consistency and plenty of praise, I have no doubt your puppy will be housebroken in no time!

What's Next..

Now that you're well on your way to having a potty-trained pup, it's time to start thinking about a more comprehensive dog training plan. Unfortunately, most pet tend to slack on training once their puppy is past the housebroken stage. But without a basic understanding of dog training do's and don'ts, pet owners may be setting up their puppy with bad habits for life.

An improperly trained dog is the number one reason so many dogs end up in shelters and why thousands of dogs are euthanized every year. That's why it's so important to train your pup the correct way, right from the start.

For that reason, I've decided to include an extra chapter that outlines **20 Biggest Dog Training Mistakes** that dog owners make when it comes to training their four-legged friends. Chances are, you will find several, if not all, apply to you and your dog either now or in the future. You will then be able to avoid or slowly erase the damage these mistakes have done to your training and begin teaching your dog the right and efficient way.

You will soon be less frustrated with your pup and have more free time to spend enjoying activities with your family and dog together. Plus you will have less stress throughout the day since you won't have to worry about how your pup will react to new people or how your house will look when you get home. By properly training your puppy and avoiding common mistakes, you can enjoy a new sense of freedom with your perfectly behaved pet.

Chapter 11:

20 Worst Dog Training Mistakes

I think we can all agree that dogs are the best companions to have by our side. They provide friendship, protection, and entertainment. But in order for you to really benefit from dog ownership, the dog needs to understand boundaries and engage in the correct behavior in order to keep all involved parties happy. There are many myths, incorrect information and training techniques floating around the dog training world that can leave owners and their dogs both confused and frustrated. It's no wonder that there is so much room for training mistakes.

A dog's role in today's family structure has changed over the years, but our training methods have not. While dogs used to have supporting roles on farms or were used for hunting or protection, they have become more of an equal member of the family today. While their previous roles required extensive training, the lifestyle of the modern dog may leave the owner thinking that minimal training is needed and they can get around to it when they are ready. There are also ancient training techniques that are still in practice today that have become irrelevant or ineffective.

With so many different options and opinions when it comes to training, many owners don't realize the mistakes that they are making and become quickly frustrated with their dog, when it is certainly not the dog's fault.

A poorly or untrained dog can wreak havoc on a household. They may be destructive towards property and cost their owners money to replace clothing, furniture or other items. Time spent outdoors can also become frustrating if their dogs bark too much or engage in other destructive behavior such as digging holes or chasing animals.

An untrained dog can also be dangerous if their disobedience leads them to harm to another person. A dog who does not behave properly can also hurt themselves if they are engaging in activities that they should not. Training is ultimately a way to protect yourself, your dog and anything or anyone else that the dog may come in contact with.

There are many different routes to take when training your dog. They all hold the basic concept that a dog's actions can provide them with rewards or with consequences. Good behavior will earn the dog some sort of treat. Undesired behavior would result in a negative consequence, or a showing of disapproval from the owner. All different types of training have different pros and cons and will not work with every owner and every dog. The way that you train your dog is up to you, but the most important thing is that you *do* train your dog and avoid employing training mistakes that can backfire on you.

The best way to view training is that it is a mutual exercise between the owner and their dog. You are not performing training on your dog but rather you and your dog are training together. This avoids the feeling of negativity that a dog may associate with your commands and also holds you accountable for your own responsibilities as a trainer.

Training your dog or puppy the right way from the beginning will save you time, money and frustration. It is also in the best interest for your dog since a properly trained dog does not experience depression, anxiety or fear during the training process or after. Your dog will lead a happy life devoid of any behavioral problems and in return be the best companion you can have during your time together.

With that being said, let's jump right in and discover some of the most common training mistakes you need to avoid.

Mistake #1: Crating Your Dog or Puppy For Long Hours

Pet owners often crate their dogs when they leave because they want to prevent the dog or puppy from having a bathroom accident in the house. While this is understandable, a crate will not prevent this from happening. A crate will not turn off your dog's bladder and eventually, the inevitable will happen. This is just how nature works. A puppy that is younger than four months can only hold their urine for a few hours at a time. If they are left in a crate all day, they will have no choice but to relieve themselves inside of it. This leads to frustration for both the owner and the puppy.

Other than physical capabilities, another reason that a dog may also soil their crate is because they have too much free space available to them. By nature, a dog will not relieve themselves near the area that they sleep. But if the dog has an oversized crate, he will think that this is acceptable and may not understand why you are upset. After all, you provided him with what he feels is a bathroom area.

The dog can also become sick if they are left in a dirty environment for too long. Dogs have been known to consume their bodily waste if it is not removed and sits near them for long periods of time, which can certainly be the case if the dog is in a crate all day. Their fur can get dirty and just like humans, dogs do not enjoy feeling unclean. This will also hinder the housebreaking process and you may find that it takes much longer than you originally anticipated to train your dog to relieve themselves outside. This can delay other areas of training and can put strain on the relationship between the owner and dog

Not only will you have quite the mess to clean up after coming home, your dog will know that you are upset. Dogs have a keen sense that enables them to know when their owners are less than happy. This creates a stressful environment for the dog, especially since their mistake is mostly out of their control.

Many dog training books will tell you it's okay to keep your dog locked up for eight hours or more when you go to work in order to protect your house from damage. But the truth is, it's not okay. In fact, it borders on cruel.

Keeping a dog in a crate all day where he can hardly move is not what one should expect of man's best friend. It can cause a dog to be lonely and experience anxiety and stress.

The Right Way To Crate

Crates are meant to imitate a dog's natural habitat. In the wild, dogs tend to seek out caves or other areas to escape from the elements. They will sleep in the den and will not soil it. However, they wouldn't stay in a den all day, so this cannot be assumed for crates either. Dogs need freedom to move as they wish. The goal of a crate should be that it becomes a place for your dog to think of as his own den and a place to seek refuge or sleep at night.

During the early months and even the first year, you will need to adjust your daily schedule to include bathroom breaks for your dog. You may need to come home during your lunch break and will have to make a stop at home before running errands after work. If you are having difficulty making it back home, you may have to seek help from other family members or friends. A dog will absolutely hold their bodily fluids if they know that a potty-break is coming. Dogs thrive on routine and will quickly adapt to a schedule with bathroom breaks throughout.

A dog should first be introduced to a crate when they are a puppy. They should learn to view the crate as a haven where they can relax and avoid any chaos in the house. With an early introduction to a crate, the puppy will grow to enjoy their secluded space, as long as it is not used as a form of punishment or captivity. As the owner, you will be able to enjoy coming home to a clean crate, dog and house.

Mistake #2: Not Taking Your Dog For Walks Because You Have a Big Yard.

Having a large yard, although nice, should not be used as an excuse for not taking your dog for walks. A walk is so much more to your dog than just a leisurely stroll down the street. It is an exciting adventure that allows your pup to explore and understand his world better.

One very important reason you need to take your dog for walks is so he can sniff stuff. A major key to understanding your dog is to understand that dogs senses differ from humans. Dogs primarily interpret the world through sense of smell whereas humans mainly rely on sight. When dogs stop to sniff something, you may assume there are simply smelling a scent, but in reality they are smelling an entire story.

You see, dogs can smell pheromones, which can be found in urine, fecal matter, skin and fur. This is what allows them to gather a lot of data about another dog or human. With a single sniff they can determine gender, mating status, what food they ate and places they've been.

When you deny your dog or puppy the opportunity to smell new things by not taking them for walks, you deny your dog the opportunity to understand the world. This can have some negative effects on your dog. For instance, some breeds of dogs, especially pointers and hound dogs, who rely heavily on their sense of smell then others, may tend to run away more often if not given the opportunity to explore their world through scent.

Exercise is also a very important reason to walk your dog. Just like humans, dogs are becoming more overweight. This is because they are allowed to lead a life with very little enforced exercise and where everything is catered to them. This leads to a very unhealthy dog and high vet bills. Daily walks will keep them healthy and allow them to live a longer and happier life.

Not providing exercise will lead to a dog having excess energy with no outlet to release it. Just because you have a large yard or plenty of dog toys to occupy your pet does not mean that they will embrace exercise on their own.

When a dog doesn't have an outlet for all of its energy, several scenarios may take place that can be viewed as the dog misbehaving. This includes excessive barking that appears to be for no reason, destructive behavior towards furniture or other household items, or the inability to sit still or stay attentive. All of these are signs that the dog has pent up energy, not that they are necessarily deliberately disobeying. If your dog is bored, he will find ways to entertain himself. This is often viewed as bad behavior but this is certainly not the dog's intention.

A dog without exercise becomes an unhealthy dog. They can gain weight that can lead to more serious internal conditions, such as stressed joints or difficulty breathing. A dog who isn't allowed to get out and explore from time to time will also become less social.

Scheduling Time For Walks

Even if you think you don't have time for daily walks, there are certainly times in your day that you can adjust to accommodate the activity. You can get up a little earlier in the morning or cut your television time down in the evening. You can turn it into an event for the whole family that will benefit everyone involved. Try to incorporate at least five walks per week, all of them lasting at least twenty minutes.

If you do find it difficult to make it outside for a walk with your dog on a certain days, see if your schedule will allow you to take him with you for some errands. You can hit the drive-through at the bank and even take your dog into certain pet stores to get his necessities for the week. You may find yourself with the time to stop at a park. If it becoming increasingly difficult to find the time for walks, you can hire a service to walk your dog for you. Avoid letting your schedule be the reason that your dog is missing out on walks. There is always a way to incorporate a walk for your dog into their daily routine.

During your walks, remember that dogs tend to spend a lot of time sniffing the ground and objects while on a walk. Do not discourage this behavior. This is a large part of a dog's make-up. Dogs can smell scents one thousand times better than we can and their sense of smell is their strongest sense. While a beautiful sunset may relax you, a walk where your dog is allowed to explore with their nose has almost the same effect on their mood. It's how they take in the scenery.

Mistake #3: Grabbing Your Dogs Collar

Some dogs, especially ones that have been adopted at a later stage in life and have unknown background stories, can

71

have a negative reaction to having their collar grabbed. This is commonly referred to as collar sensitivity. Dog owners can make the mistake of classifying this as bad behavior when really it needs to be dealt with in a much different way.

If you typically put your dog or puppy in a crate or bring him inside from playtime by pulling on his collar, it won't take long for him to associate this action with the end of fun time. They will quickly learn to fight it. A dog will also remember when their collar is grabbed in a way that may seem aggressive. This can be dangerous because your hand is close to their mouth.

A dog's natural instincts could eventually lead them to nip at you or someone else. This can be especially dangerous if children pull on the dog's collar because they've seen it done before. Almost twenty percent of dog bites occur when a dog's collar is being grabbed.

Pulling a dog's collar can appear to be an attack from their point of view, which is understandable. Imagine if someone suddenly grabbed your shirt collar as you were walking. You would most likely take it as a threat. It can also be painful and can cause damage to the dog's throat if done hard enough. If he decides to fight back, it can also lead to the owner getting injured.

A dog owner shouldn't solely rely on the collar as a means to control their dog or get their dog's attention. Your main focus during training should be teaching your dog or puppy verbal commands.

How To Cure Collar Sensitivity

The best way to combat collar sensitivity is to teach the dog that good things can happen when their collar is grabbed and that it is not always done with aggressive intentions. Start by giving the dog several small rewards, such as verbal praise or an edible treat, without touching their collar.

If the dog remains calm, take one hand and pat the top of their head while using the other hand to feed them a treat. Move your hand to the dog's chin and simultaneously feed them treats. Keep moving your hands toward the collar and eventually grab it, all while giving the dog treats and verbal praise. Keep these training sessions short, but once you have successfully completed five to ten sessions, you should be able to grab the dog's collar when it is necessary without doing any damage to their psyche.

Instead of grabbing your dog by the collar to get him into his crate, try to coax him in gently by throwing a treat towards the back. If you must clip the dog's nails or wash their paws, call the dog or use a command to get their attention. Reward them for listening and cooperating after the task is finished. Do not hold them throughout the process by their collar.

If your dog has a strong sensitivity to the collar and displays tendencies to nip or bite, remember that your safety comes first. Start wearing protective gloves or use a muzzle to prevent injury. Stay consistent with reassurance, and protective gear will soon no longer be required.

Mistake #4: Jerking Back on Your Dog or Puppy's Leash

When your dog sees another canine at the park or while out on a walk, their first reaction may be to jump towards the other dog, probably barking at the same time. They may feel threatened by the other dog and their fight or flight response will automatically kick in. Since they cannot run away, they feel that their only option is to make their presence known and be prepared to fight for their safety and defend their territory.

Your first reaction might be to jerk back on the leash,

attempting to stop the altercation. One problem with this mistake is that it can seriously harm the dog, especially if their collar doesn't fit right or if you are using a choke collar. The main problem with this mistake is that it is no way a form of training. It may stop the dog for the moment, but the next time they see another dog while they are out, they most certainly will still jump and become defensive, causing you to jerk the leash again.

Nothing about jerking the leash will teach your dog that their actions are unnecessary and undesirable, but it may lead them to think that other dogs are bad, since there is a consequence when they see one. This will make your dog anti-social over time and it will be harder for them to be around other dogs and people in the future.

If you keep jerking the leash every time your dog lashes out during a walk, nothing productive will come out of it. If the owner pulls too hard on the leash, the dog may be seriously hurt. If the owner pulls too soft, the dog may think that it is some sort of game and will jump and pull even more. While there is a degree that you can safely pull the leash that may get the dog to stop what they are doing, it is not an effective training method.

Jerking back on the leash sends serious mixed signals to your dog. They are already nervous because they see another dog and are uncertain of what to do. While they are experiencing this anxiety, their owner can make them feel even more anxious or upset when they pull the leash. A dog should enjoy their walk but it has now turned into a less than desirable experience and one that your dog may want to avoid in the future. Your dog may also learn that it is best to just avoid other people or dogs but this is unhealthy behavior.

Socializing Your Dog On A Leash

The best way to handle this situation is to teach the dog to not be afraid of other dogs in the first place, even though it is a natural fear for domesticated dogs. Slowly begin introducing them to other dogs, either on walks or at the park. This gentle introduction to other dogs will help your dog get over their natural fear of the unknown as they realize that there is no real threat to them.

Until your dog learns how to walk without tugging, consider each walk a training session. This means that you need to stay consistent. Before you go on walks, spend some time exercising with the dog beforehand. Play fetch or run around the yard for a bit. The less excess energy that the dog has, the less likely they will be to pull forward on the leash or get excited if they see something new. Use rewards to show the dog that you approve of well behaved walks.

If you are just beginning to introduce your dog to a leash, there are some tips you can use to help the dog adjust. After clipping on the dog's leash, allow them some time to get used to the feel of it. Let them run around the yard without you holding onto it, supervising for any danger of tangling. Begin by just walking around the yard, in different unpredictable patterns.

Whenever your dog stays near you, reward him with a treat. Once you feel that your dog is ready, start taking walks through the neighborhood or at a park. As your dog improves, lessen the amount of edible treats and continue with verbal praise. While you are allowed to keep the leash tight as a reminder to the dog that you are holding it, never allow yourself to pull on the leash as a means of moving the dog or stopping them from jumping forward.

Mistake # 5: Training Dogs Through Punishment

Some trainers today still recommend using punishment as a way to stop your dog's bad behavior. While this used to be a normal and accepted technique of dog training, it has been shown to usually cause more harm than positive training results. If anything, it delays the dog from learning desired behaviors. Using any form of punishment can lead to an increase in aggression in the dog. Different types of punishment include sudden jerks on a leash, physically hitting or kicking the dog, forcing the dog into a submissive position, spraying the dog with water or excessive shouting and yelling. If the dog finds the incident to be unpleasant, it can be considered a form of punishment.

Studies have shown that children who were spanked as a form of discipline were twice as likely to develop aggressive behaviors as they grew older. A dog usually displays the same mental process as a toddler, so the same type of violent punishment is likely to have the same outcome of aggression. All dogs personalities differ from each other, so punishment can have different effects on different dogs. For example, a dog who is more sensitive than most may suffer from low self esteem and be wary of people. The same dog will also become depressed and will be unable to learn through any type of training since it may be scared of his owner. A dog that is a little more naturally tough will not likely be bothered emotionally by physical punishment but will certainly associate the punishment with fear and may fight back one day, turning a once nice dog into a danger.

If you feel the need to punish your dog after misbehaving, this is a clear sign that your current training techniques are not working. Your dog is still misbehaving and punishing them will only push the training progress backwards. Your dog may only learn from each punishment that their owner is mean and they should fear them. Dogs learn best by being shown what is expected of them and then being rewarded when they do it.

Positive Training

Now that we know the serious side effects of using a technique involving punishments to train your dog, it can easily be said that doing the opposite will have much more positive results. This is known as positive reinforcement and is highly recommended by dog training experts today. Instead of bringing negative attention to your dogs misbehavior, reward their good behavior through either edible treats, extra play time or verbal praise. This will motivate the dog to continue the favored behavior and abandon the behavior that didn't provide a reward.

The reward should happen immediately after the dog has displayed good behavior or followed a command. This way the dog will know exactly what he is being rewarded for. If you are teaching your dog to sit, yelling the command while pushing down on his bottom will provide your dog with a very negative experience that most likely won't provide you with any training results. He will want to avoid this situation in the future and it certainly won't teach him how to sit any faster. If you approach the training session enthusiastically and wait until your dog sits, rewarding him will keep him happy and focused on the training. This training will require a little more patience on your part, but you should reach your final training goal much quicker. Your dog will want to continue learning and will enjoy training sessions.

Children also learn better in a positive and rewarding environment compared to a hostile and negative one. Imagine what kind of work environment you would want to be in. It most likely involves positive reinforcement. Keep this same mentality in mind when training your dog and provide them with a positive and safe learning environment.

Mistake #6: Not Rewarding Your Pup Enough For Good Behavior

Dogs live in the moment. If you do not reward your dog quickly for good behavior, the dog will remember that their actions did not please you. A reward should be issued within a few seconds after an act of good behavior and make logical sense to the dog. For example, if you are teaching your dog to stay and you only reward the dog after you have allowed the dog to move again, the dog thinks that they are being rewarded for moving. A reward does not always need to be an edible treat. A happy tone of voice and a reassuring phrase is sometimes all that a dog needs to know that they have done something right.

This is a common mistake and usually happens farther into training. A dog that was doing well and following commands will suddenly stop. This is because they have stopped receiving any kind of praise and no longer have motivation.

Dogs depend on structure and routine. They will look to their owner to provide this. If you only reward a dog when you have time or when you feel like it, they will become confused and will most likely abandon their learned commands and behaviors without your positive reinforcement.

Sometimes dogs can view your responses as rewards when that is not your intention. For example, if you give in to your dog barking for your attention, they will view your shift of attention towards them as a reward. This will cause them to bark again when they want you to play with them or stop whatever it is that you may be doing. Anything that makes your dog happy is considered to be a reward so make sure that your actions speak the right attitude towards your dog's behavior. This is why it is so important to remain consistent and focused during training.

Reward Training

When you are first training your puppy or dog, it is recommended to use treats. Make sure that the treats you are using are ones that your dog truly enjoys. Try a few different ones until you find one that they can't resist. The food should be soft and able to be eaten quickly and not something that the dog needs to chew on for several minutes. Just as your giving the reward should be quick, so should the consumption. This keeps the dog living in the moment. When giving the dog a treat, follow it immediately with a positive phrase that the dog will associate with approval.

You do not want to have to give your dog a treat every single time they sit or listen to a command for their whole life though. An effective technique to follow when training your dog with treats goes as follows. When you are first teaching the dog a new command, reward them every time that they successfully complete it. After a while, lessen the treats to four out of every five times and slowly decrease the number of treats until they only happen occasionally. However, still use the associated positive phrase every time the dog displays correct behavior. The dog will learn to look for this phrase more than food, but they will still appreciate the extra snack from time to time.

A dog will be pleased with an enthusiastic response from you or even a few minutes of petting them and a little extra attention. By continuing to give your dog verbal praise, your dog will enjoy pleasing you, especially when he knows that on occasion he will receive an edible treat. This will keep your dog motivated and happy.

Mistake #7: Not Establishing Family Rules

This can be a common mistake for families that have not established a set of rules and guidelines for training their dog. A dog may be scolded for an action by one family member and the same action will receive no reaction from another. This can cause the dog to have a negative opinion of the first family member and cause the dog to possibly fear them. If one family member is using one word for a command and another family member has chosen a different word for the same command, the dog will become confused and possibly not respond to either word. All of this leads to a frustrating environment for both the dog and the family.

Training is based on repetitiveness, so when there are changes to the system, the process and everyone involved loses integrity. A dog will pick up on this very fast. If a dog loses faith with their owners, it will cause a string of events leading to more bad behavior. This can all be avoided by consistent training, both in wording and intensity.

If inconsistent training is allowed to continue in your household, the dog will never become fully trained. He will become frustrated and lose interest in training because the overall experience is tiring and unproductive. The family will also lose interest in training. A large percentage of dogs that are given up for adoption are dogs who are considered to be incapable of progressing during training. All dogs are trainable but sometimes owners give up, not realizing that it is their own mistakes that are hindering the dog's progress.

All family members should be using the same commands and training methods in order to prevent slowing down the training process for a dog. It may help to keep a list of all the commands being taught to the dog in a place that is easily accessible and seen every day. Also, keep a list of all the rules for the dog. If the dog is not allowed on the couch, the dog will not learn this if one member of the family still allows them on the furniture when no one else is home.

Not only will this be problematic for the dog, it can also cause arguments and tension between the family members. In order to provide the best training and living environment for your dog, the whole family will need to sit down and have a meeting about training. During this meeting, the family should establish the commands that they will use and how they will handle behavioral issues. There will most likely be some areas where there will need to be compromise but just remember to keep the dog's best interest in mind.

Part of training your dog is training yourself too. You cannot take a day off from training. Each good behavior should be rewarded and each bad behavior should be properly attended to. This is part of the reason why training is a mutual activity. Especially when a family unit is responsible for training a dog, extra steps need to be taken before training even starts to make sure that everyone is on the same page.

Mistake #8: Pushing Your Puppy's Nose in Household Mistakes

During potty training and sometimes even after, dogs can have accidents. They might also get into the garbage, rip apart a couch cushion or chew your favorite shoes when you aren't home. When you walk in the door, your first instinct might be to punish the dog. However, there is a right way and a wrong way to handle these types of situations. How you handle it will make all the difference in its likelihood to happen again or not.

Remember that dogs live in the moment. Therefore, in order for them to be effective, the consequences for their actions need to happen immediately, whether good or bad. This means that you also need to have actually seen what they have done for them to earn their consequence. So if something happened at home while you were not there, you simply can't punish the dog for it. Punishment when you get home will teach the dog to be scared of you, since you are unpredictable in their eyes and they won't be able to associate your anger with their past actions. This can cause anxiety and depression in the dog and certainly won't stop the negative behavior.

Some owners think that their dog is acting guilty or hiding from them when they come home to a mess. Dogs do not have the capability to decipher between right and wrong, even though many owners think that they do. Any act from a dog that displays remorse is simply a memory of previous consequences. For example, it was fun the last time that they chewed on your shoe but since you caught them right away and dealt with the situation, they remember the unpleasantness.

Chewing up a shoe and not getting caught is just as much fun as the first time, but now they know the following consequences are coming. This has nothing to do with thinking that chewing on the shoe was wrong. This is why it is important to only display disapproval when you catch your dog in the act. Otherwise they will associate the displeasure as something that happens when you come home instead of in relation to disobedience.

Puppy Proofing

This is a situation where it's important to understand that training is a mutual experience. You will need to take precautions for times when you aren't home. Try to keep the garbage in a place that they can't reach it and make sure that you aren't leaving your dog for longer than their system can hold waste. You can work on stopping the dog from chewing cushions and clothing when you are home, but when you aren't home close doors and add gates to keep the dog from areas where they may destroy the house. If you are gone for short period of time, you may want to consider using a crate. Providing your dog with a safe environment where they have the chance to succeed in being well behaved goes a long way.

With the proper combination of training and handling undesirable situations the right way, your dog will soon be able to be home alone for several consecutive hours without any problems. But remember, if your puppy has a bad day and an accident occurs, deal with it correctly and don't let your anger take over.

If your dog is older and having accidents in the house, make sure to have the dog checked by a veterinarian to make sure there are no health issues present.

Mistake #9: Not Training Puppy On Day 1

This is such a common mistake and most new dog owners are guilty of it. By the time you adopt a dog, they are absolutely old enough to begin training immediately. Just because your puppy is still in a cute and playful stage does not mean that they are incapable of some beginning stages of training. Puppies actually look for a leader and the first person that they will turn to is you. They want someone to help guide them and provide stability in their lives. Don't wait until your dog is older or until their behavior becomes a problem.

Every day that you let go by without training is another day that the dog may be learning negative behaviors. If a dog is allowed to go so long without being reprimanded, it will be that much harder to enforce proper behavior. If you think that you are not training your dog yet, this means that you are training your dog in negative behavior and teaching him that there are no consequences for his actions.

If you have waited an excessive amount of time to start your training, it is not too late. You may have more obstacles ahead of you and your dog may be slightly confused as to what brought on the new discipline but you can still be successful in your training, despite your dogs age or current behavioral issues.

Start Training Today

The first step to fixing this mistake is to start training right away. This training must be consistent. If you have let your dog engage in improper behavior for several months or even years, you will need to completely break your own habits before you can expect the dog to catch on. This is where the mentality of training being a group exercise comes into play. You are going through just as much training as your dog is right now and it may be frustrating at times. Learn from your own frustration and know that your dog is feeling the same way. Avoid getting upset with your dog during this transitional period.

There is a right way and a wrong way to introduce your puppy to training. Housebreaking your puppy will be one of the first parts of training that you incorporate into their lives. Once your dog is mostly house trained, this is a great time to start introducing some more advanced training. Keep training sessions short or your dog may become bored and will stop responding. An ideal time frame for training is fifteen minutes.

A puppy can learn simple commands once they are one month old but you will see better results as they grow. Avoid moving on to new commands if a puppy is still struggling with the first few that you have introduced.

This is a great time to emphasize that every dog trains a little different. Don't take a bump in the road as a sign that your dog cannot be trained. It just means that you might have to look into different techniques to continue advancing in dog training. Do not give up; your dog will thank you for it!

Mistake #10: Reassuring Your Puppy When He is Fearful

Most dogs will cower with fear during a loud

thunderstorm or when there are fireworks and other loud and sudden noises. This leads to a very common mistake among owners as they reach out to comfort their dog. We are concerned for our dog and want to take the fear away, which is a natural reaction to have. But cuddling only shows the dog that their fear is justified and will not prevent the fear during the next storm. It will encourage it. Dogs have emotions just like people do and one of them is fear. Just as a child may be fearful of a thunderstorm, dogs can be too. They might be scared of any sudden and loud noises that may occur. These loud noises can cause stress and anxiety for your dog, including an elevated heart rate and intense breathing. It is very normal, especially since dogs have a higher sensitivity to sounds than humans do. While there are some acceptable levels of reassurance that you can give to a dog during these stressful periods, eventually they will need to be taught that there is nothing for them to fear. If you coddle them every time there is thunder or something that is not dangerous that causes them fear, they will never understand that there is nothing to be scared of.

If a dog is reassured with each new storm, not only will this allow the behavior to continue, it will most likely make it worse. The first storm may make the dog nervous. The tenth may cause the dog to have a dangerous panic attack, where they bark or become suddenly aggressive, chew their own skin enough to break through, shake uncontrollably and have a dangerously high heart rate. By enabling the fear, you are allowing possible harm to come to your dog.

If the habit is not broken, it will also interfere with your own schedule. If there is a storm when you are not home, you may feel the need to rush to your dog's side and comfort them. While a dog certainly relies on their owner, they need to be able to function alone as well.

Don't Validate Fear

While it is human nature to want to comfort and end a dog's fear, certain reassurances that you may give will only teach them that their fears are validated. So while you shouldn't simply ignore the situation, don't bring more attention to it than it deserves. If you do ignore it, the fear will most likely increase in the dog rather than disappear. The most important thing to do is stay calm. This will show your dog that the noises or commotion that they are hearing is nothing to be scared of. Keep in mind that dogs can sense the onset of a thunderstorm, so you may notice anxious activity before the first clap of thunder.

Praise calm behavior with verbal praise or even a treat. You can try to distract the dog with some extra play time or a new toy. If your dog has a crate or special dog bed that they find comforting, make this available to them. There are even special shirts and wraps on the market that are designed to reduce anxiety in dogs, just as a blanket for a baby would do.

If you live in an area that only has thunderstorms during certain parts of the year, keep your dog used to the noises by playing thunder noises for them during the off season. This will prevent them from forgetting all of their calming techniques that have been learned during the storm season. Do not be surprised if a dog that never feared storms suddenly gets nervous when they hear thunder. This can happen without warning in some dogs.

By teaching your dog calming techniques, you can be assured that your dog will be able to get through a storm, even if you are not home. This will be beneficial to you both.

Mistake #11: Not Providing a Dog or Puppy with Chew Toys.

It may not seem like a big deal, but providing your dog or

puppy with the right kind of chew toy is crucial his to growth and development. Chewing is actually more important than most pet owners realize. For starters, it's a way for young pups to explore their environment. From the time your puppy is just a couple of months old, you can pretty much expect that he will begin testing out his newly-grown teeth on objects within his immediate surroundings.

Just like a toddler might go from room to room, picking up anything and everything not nailed to the floor, your pup is going to put his mouth on most anything he comes into contact with. Not much is off limits when it comes to your puppy's chewing preferences. You name it -- shoes, furniture, remote controls or even underwear (hey, it happens) -- are all fair game when it comes to a curious pup.

There are a wide range of benefits for giving your puppy the right kind of chew toy. The most obvious benefit is the fact that if your little pup has his (or her) own designated chew toy, he is going to be a whole lot less likely to chew on your slippers instead.

To keep your sanity and your cool, you'll need to redirect your puppy's chewing habits. This means getting a safe chew toy and redirecting his attention to it and away from something of value. This becomes especially important if your puppy is "teething." As a puppy's teeth begin to break the surface of the gums, not only will they be greatly aided if he has something to chew on, but gnawing on hard objects will give him relief from any pain he may feel during the process. It also provides him with just the right kind of pressure to help his teeth come forth.

As your pup grows into an adult, chewing hard objects like bones becomes of vital importance to his oral and dental health care because it aids the scraping of harmful plaque and tartar buildup from his teeth. It can also help prevent gingivitis and periodontal disease later in life. In essence, chewing for dogs is the equivalent of us humans brushing our teeth. So in order to avoid a very expensive bill from your vet to have your dog's teeth professionally scraped, make sure you take the time to provide your pet with an appropriate chew toy.

Choosing a Safe Chew Toy

There are many types of chew toys to give your dog, from rawhide to nylon. There are also some positives and negatives to think about depending on your dogs age—so which one is the best choice? And even more importantly, which one is safest?

For starters, you want to make sure the toy is hard enough so that your dog can't chew off small pieces and possibly choke on them. For this reason, Nylabones are a popular item among dog owners. They are made of tough material and are great for adult dogs. Because they help scrape off plaque as they chew. However they can be harmful for young puppies whose teeth and chewing capacity are still developing. A puppy's teeth may not be strong enough yet to handle the hardness of the bone. Giving puppy's something as hard and unwieldy as a Nylabone may not be the best choice until their teeth are fully developed .

Puppies begin the process of teething a few months after birth. It is at this stage in their growth, that their little "puppy teeth" get an upgrade and the first new "adult teeth" begin to come in. The first of the puppy's baby teeth to come undone are usually the incisors—the sharp little teeth pups use for cutting and tearing their food. Dog's usually have about 12 of these teeth so don't be alarmed if you find a pair or two on your floor, or the cushion of your couch. Losing baby teeth is just a part of your pup's process of growing up.

It's also right around this time that your puppy will begin actively looking for items to chew on. As mentioned in the previous section, it's up to you as their caregiver, to give your puppy dog something that they can *safely chew on*. Puppy teething typically lasts until the dog is about 6 months of age, by then all of the animal's adult teeth should be in, and a proper chewing routine should be established.

Certain real bones can be a hazard as well. Cooked bones, especially from poultry, can splinter and cut open a pup's mouth or worse yet, the animal could swallow the jagged edges. If you like the idea of giving your dog real bones, get raw beef bones from the butcher. Not only will the marrow provide your dog with the extra nutrients he needs, but they are basically indestructible. Make sure to avoid poultry and pork bones altogether. Wait until your puppy's teeth are fully developed before you introduce him to raw bones.

You also want to make sure not to give your puppy a "stuffed squeaky toy". These toys have parts that a curious puppy could get a hold of and choke on. Solid rubber chew toys are your best bet. They are very basic because and usually made of one material; plus, the rubber makes them ultra durable. Among the better rubber chew toys on the market right now are the popular "Kong" chew toys. These toys are usually hollow in the middle, allowing you the option of adding dog food or other treats inside to keep your pet's attention.

Mistake #12: Not Socializing Your Dog Early Enough

Many people make the mistake of not properly socializing their pets with both humans and other dogs right from the get go. A properly socialized dog understands that not all strangers and animals are a threat. Socializing your dog at a young age will help prevent him from developing bad habits that can present themselves later on. More often than not, dogs who are not socialized properly as a puppy have a hard time dealing with stressful social situations compared to dogs who were.

Poor socialization skills can result in bad habits such dogs being either aggressive or jumping all over visitors as soon as they enter the front door. If your pup is never exposed to proper social interaction, he will let loose with unbridled hyperactive energy any way he sees fit. And while it might initially seem cute that your puppy jumps with energetic joy when you come home, by the time he is full grown and capable of knocking over your unsuspecting guests—it's really not all that endearing.

That's why it's important to start socializing your pup as early as possible. That said, puppies a little over 12 weeks are ready to be socialized. At this age, pups become more curious and begin to more fully use their senses, as they investigate their surroundings. Prior to 12 weeks old, your puppy may be more fearful than curious, canceling out any desire to interact with the environment. However, from 12 weeks all the way to 3 months, the desire to be social will be greater than the tendency to be frightened.

At this point in your dog's development, they are the most open to "new experiences." If during this crucial time, he is not trained with proper socialization when encountering something new—such as a house guest or another dog—he may retreat back into a more fearful disposition, leading to potentially life-long anxiety and aggression.

Like anything, proper socialization requires patience and a lot of trial and error. Your pup has to learn through experience what is expected of him in social situations. And when your pup manages to get it right, you need to reward him. This reward for proper social conduct can be a gentle pat or a simple, soothing praise of, "Good dog!" As with any training, positive reinforcement is crucial.

If for example, your pup manages to calmly greet visitors to your home without jumping all over them, you need to let them know you are pleased with how they handled that social situation. While socializing your dog or puppy with other dogs, allow them to first observe other animals at play. Stay a far enough distance away so that he does not react. If he acts calm and without aggression when another dog comes near praise him or give him a treat.

For most dogs, the quickest way to their heart is through their stomachs. So, handing them a tasty treat, coupled with a nice round of verbal praise and perhaps an affectionate pat on the back, should be sufficient to let them know that they had chosen their behavior wisely, and their good behavior will be rewarded.

This will create a positive feedback loop for a dog who is seeking to impress you with his good socialization skills to get approval. For a dog, one of their greatest drives in life is to win the approval and esteem of his owner.

Mistake #13: Reactively Training Your Dog

Another big mistake that pet owners make is "reactively training" their dog or puppy. Reactive training is when you attempt to correct your dog's behavior as an immediate, adverse reaction to something he has done. If, for example, you come home from work and find that your pup has relieved himself on the rug, your initial response may be to become angry and punish him on the spot. This is a major no-no. You have to think from a dog's perspective. Even though your dog's accident may be fresh in your mind because you just got home, your dog has most likely forgotten all about it and has no idea why you are freaking out.

From your pup's point of view, he will simply perceive you coming home angry for no apparent reason. So, by reacting to something he did several hours after the fact, he will most likely not get the connection and will not understand why you are punishing him. In fact, you will only succeed in making your pup afraid of you. Only attempt to correct him when you catch him in the act. If you suddenly see him squatting on your living room floor, you can quickly shout out a firm, "No! Bad dog!" and he will immediately associate your displeasure with the attempt at an indoor bathroom break. Then calmly lead him to your approved potty-training area.

While corrective training is necessary at times, proactively training your dog is a much more effective method because it helps prevent the bad behavior from happening in the first place. With proactive training, you are anticipating your dog's response before the behavior happens which allows you to correct the behavior before the fact.

One way you can accomplish this is by controlling your pups immediate environment. For example, if your puppy is peeing all over the house then it's a good indication he has too much freedom to roam and he should be limited to certain areas. And instead of having to correct your pup for gnawing on the furniture after-the-fact, simply restrict his access to areas of the house with furniture when he is not being supervised. By restricting your dog's choices to exhibit bad behavior, you are setting him up for future success.

Just as you would restrict a toddler's access to a hot stove or household cleaning items, you need to restrict your dog or puppy's access to things that can get him into trouble. By taking a proactive approach to your training, you take responsibility for your pet's behavior right from the beginning.

Mistake #14: Yelling or Raising Your Voice

As you know already or about to find out, dog training can at times be extremely frustrating. It can lead to occasions where you find yourself tempted to yell or raise your voice when correcting your pup's behavior. And more often than not, yelling only increases a dog's excitement and anxiety levels. Yelling may make you feel better initially but it usually fails to curtail unwanted behavior.

Remember, dogs have better hearing than humans, so if they don't listen to us at a normal volume level, raising your voice isn't likely to do much good either. What will do some good, however, is immediate corrective action coupled with a firm and carefully worded command. If, for example, your dog attempts to lunge at other animals in the park as you go for a walk, you are probably tempted to scream at the top of your lungs, "come back here right now!", instead you should calmly but firmly lead your dog in the opposite direction and issue a simple command such as "no".

Calm and corrective action will gain your dog's attention much more effectively than frantic screaming. It's simply the way dogs are wired. Dogs are far more likely to follow the commands of a calm and resolute leader than a screaming maniac. Pet owners have a tendency to treat their dogs like children, not to say that you should be screaming at a child. But there is often a major disconnect between a dog and its owner when it comes to how the pet interprets loud vocalizations.

For instance, if your dog lunges at a squirrel and you just start screaming, Get back! Get back!'" your dog may interpret your excitement as, "Get him! Get him!" It's important to remember that while dogs may understand some words, they are not native English speakers. Canines can sense your mood and body language. So, if you are expressing alarm and excitement, your dog will too.

You want to make sure you are not adding more chaos and confusion to a situation. Instead of yelling, just calmly issue a simple command such as "stop" or "no" in a flat, firm tone of voice and a quick tug on his leash. This will quickly get his attention, and snap him out of his misbehavior.

Mistake #15 Command Nagging

Command nagging is when a dog does not respond to a pet owner's cue the very first time, so you end up repeating yourself until the dog obeys. One reason your dog may not respond initially is because you failed to properly gain his attention before issuing the command.

If your dog is distracted and busy doing something else when you suddenly shout a command like, "Come here!", you may find it only causes your dog to look up from whatever he was doing with a puzzled look. You want to make sure that you already have your dog's undivided attention before the command is issued. Don't make the mistake of trying to get your dog's attention with the command rather than beforehand. Otherwise, you find yourself repeating your commands and teaching your dog that he does not have to respond to the first command.

There are several things you can do to gain your dog's attention first. You could whistle or snap your fingers before issuing a command. When you have your dog's full attention, he is better prepared to heed your instructions the very first time around.

For example, let's say you see your dog chewing on a house plant. No problem. Just whistle, snap your fingers, clap your hands, stomp on the floor—do whatever you can to get your pup's attention. Once he makes eye contact, you now have his full attention and can issue your command.

Another reason your dog may not respond to a command right away is because he associates it with something negative. If every time you command your dog to "come here", for the purpose of giving him a bath or to scold him, he will associate that command with something he dislikes. It's imperative that your commands are positively reinforced, especially when your dog is learning the commands for the first time.

Mistake #16: Treating Your Dog Like a Human

It may seem a rather obvious statement, but your dog is not a human and you shouldn't be treating him like one or expect him to behave like one. I'm not saying don't love and treat him like a family member, but projecting human traits onto a dog can be detrimental -- especially for him.

By humanizing your dog, you can cause miscommunication that results in behavioral problems down the road.

Dogs in their natural state are much more impulsive than humans and do not have the same kind of cautious judgment. If he did, he wouldn't do things like drinking out of the toilet or chewing on the television cord.

Dogs don't think like us either. They learn and engage in their own unique way. In order to train your pup well, you need to reach him at his own level. It is well known that dogs exhibit a pack mentality and will establish an hierarchy of position within that pack. By treating your pup as a human, you may inadvertently allow him to establish dominance over you which can seriously hamper your training efforts.

Pet owners also tend to project human emotions onto their dogs. Many owners fall into the trap of viewing their dog's bad behavior as a deliberate act of vengeance, thinking the dog is 'getting back' at his owner in some way. For example, you may mistakenly attribute your dog's peeing on the rug as an act of spite because you left him alone when, in reality, it was really because he was feeling anxious. It's important to keep in mind that dogs do not rationalize or obsess. They live in the moment and act mainly by instinct.

One of the main reasons we like to make our pets more human than they are is to better relate to them. But there is really no need to humanize our dogs in order to appreciate them. It's better you understand your pup's innate tendencies so you can better improve your communications. Then you can truly appreciate dog for exactly who he is.

Mistake #17: Allowing Your Dog to Pull You on Walks

Out of all the dog mistakes owners make, allowing the dog to pull on his leash is probably the most annoying to dog owners. But unfortunately, it's very common. How many times have you gone to the local park and seen someone practically dragged down the street by a dog who is way out in front of them? It may look comical to the observer, but the fact is, the owner is reinforcing the bad behavior.

There are many reasons why dogs will pull on their leashes. One reason dogs pull is simply because they walk faster than humans. Many dog breeds have a long history of being bred as either hunting, herding or retrieving dogs where speed is a necessity. But probably a more simplistic answer is that dogs have four legs where humans only two, so naturally their gait is going to be much faster than ours.

Most leash pulling problems are due to a dog's excitement level. He may get excited when he sees his friends, goes to his favorite park, sees a squirrel or just exploring all the new smells. Many owners make the mistake of thinking they need to teach their dog not to pull on the leash when, in fact, they should be teaching their dog how to stay calm in certain situations.

It's important to make sure your dog is calm right from the get go. Many dogs go berserk just from hearing the jingle of their leash. Naturally, your dog associates latching the leash onto their collar with going outside, causing him to become overly excited at the prospect, to the point that he stops listening.

It's critical at this point that before you step one foot out the door, that his behavior is corrected immediately. You must make it clear to your dog that you will not take him out unless he calms down enough for you to attach the leash. If your dog starts jumping and excitedly moving about when you approach him with the leash, immediately step back and firmly ask him to sit.

Then wait a little bit and bring the leash out again. If he continues this bad behavior as you reach for the collar, step away again and command, "Sit". Do not confuse this method with the previously discussed "command nagging". Unlike "command nagging" that uselessly repeats a command word over and over, this method entails clarifying your desired intention by repeating an entire exercise until your dog clearly understands what he needs to do. Eventually, your pup will realize that his ticket out the door is to sit calmly any time you reach for his leash.

It's a good idea to initially keep your dog on a short leash, reining him in to where he has no choice but to walk beside you. Carrying a few of his favorite treats with you that can be rewarded once he falls into step with you will be extremely effective here as well. As you exit the door to take your dog outside, keep your dog to your left.

Use coercive tugs of the leash when necessary to keep the dog at your side. When he begins to walk beside you, give him a dog treat to let him know that you approve of his behavior. Do this a few times and soon he will soon naturally learn to walk beside you rather than in front of you, regardless of whether he is rewarded with a treat or not.

Mistake#18: Not Being Consistent With Training

No one likes inconsistencies, especially your dog. Dogs are creatures of habit. They live in a world of absolutes. Either you absolutely want them to sit down on command or you don't. Either you absolutely do not want them to bark at the neighbors or you do—for them there is no in between. But to us humans, it may be a bit more nuanced than that. Take, for example, the dog owner who allows his over excited dog to jump all over him when he comes home from work and then rewards the act by giving his dog hugs and praise.

However, the next day when that same owner almost gets knocked down by his excited pup, the owner then attempts to correct the dog which only causes the dog to be confused. This inconsistent discipline does not make sense for a canine. If you don't want your dog to do something, you have to remain constant with your training.

There can't be gray area in which some things are okay but on other days they are not. You need to be consistently clear in your expectations every day. You also need to use consistency with the way you word your commands. Dogs prefer to respond to the same exact phrases for specific actions rather than a wide variety of words and expressions. For example, if you start off training your dog to come by calling, "come here", but then suddenly change to, "get over here", your dog can become confused, and you may end up mistaking his confusion for disobedience.

It's also important to establish a set of family "house rules" with respect to your training. Everyone in your household needs to be on the same page about what's acceptable dog behavior and what's not. If one family member allows the dog to jump all over him or her without correcting the pet, or worse yet perhaps encouraging him to jump, the dog will become confused and not know what is expected of him. I think we can all agree that it's not fair to your dog to be corrected by one family member for doing something and encouraged by another. It's also important that everyone in the family uses the same verbal cues when training.

Consistency is a vital key to training success. Consistency of tone, consistency of commands, and consistency of action all play a major role in training your pup to be a responsible and well-mannered canine citizen.

Mistake #19: Giving Too Much Affection At The Wrong Times

The #1 reason people decide to get a dog is usually for companionship, so it's only natural that we all want to lavish love and affection on our pets. While it may sound contradictory, there can be times when too much affection -- especially if it is given at the wrong times -- can be detrimental to your training and your dog's overall behavior.

When it comes to giving your pup affection and praise, it needs to done at the correct times. Affection is an effective form of positive reinforcement and is intrinsically grafted into almost all aspects of training. In order for affection to remain such a powerful means of positive reinforcement, it needs to be given in moderation and at the right time.

When affection is given at the wrong time, you can render your means of positive reinforcement completely ineffective. Anytime you give your dog affection, you are basically reinforcing a certain behavior either in that moment or the moment directly preceding it. You are essentially telling your dog that he did something praiseworthy. For example, if your dog has a habit of jumping all over you whenever you walk through the front door and you shower him with hugs and kisses, you are reinforcing his bad behavior of jumping. Make sure you only reward affection when your dog is in a calm and submissive state.

By the same token, if you try to soothe your dog when he is experiencing anxiety, you will only succeed in reinforcing his fear. Many dog owners make the mistake of trying to comfort their dogs when's there's a thunderstorm or fireworks. The best thing you can do in these situations is to act normal and pretend that nothing is out of the ordinary.

Being overly affectionate can also lead to behavioral problems such as an overly possessive and jealous dog who views other people and animals as rivals for your attention. This could lead to aggressive behavior when other people or animals approach you. A jealous dog may even challenge your spouse if he tries to hug or snuggle with you or he may attack another animal for just being near you.

In order to prevent your dog from potentially becoming aggressive to others in the future, you need to stop rewarding his bad behavior. For example, if you are sitting on the couch and your pooch tries to come between you and another person, either say a command indicating he must get down from the couch or simply stand up and walk away without acknowledging him.

Another problem that can arise from being overly affectionate is that a dog can develop separation anxiety. Many pet owners find out the hard way that "spoiling" their pooches with love can cause them to become less independent. Some dogs can become completely unhinged whenever their owner leaves them by themselves and, unfortunately, these are the dogs most likely to end up in a shelter. By not lavishing your dog or puppy with constant attention, you'll actually be teaching him how to become a more independent and relaxed animal, even when you are not right by his side.

Mistake #20: Underestimating Your Dog's Training Ability

We've all heard the saying that an old dog can't learn new tricks, except, it's simply not true. You *can* train an older dog plenty of new things. Sure, it may take longer for older dogs to learn new things but that's mainly due to the fact that you have the added task of having to un-train the unwanted behavior first.

To prove their theory that old dogs *can* learn new tricks, the University of Veterinary Medicine in Vienna conducted a study that involved 145 border collies from as young as 6 months to up to 14 years. They tested to see how the dogs responded to both objects and people. While the older dogs did lose interest in objects faster than the younger dogs, they did maintain the same level of interest when there was a human actively involved with the object. The study concluded that even though it took longer to train older dogs, once they did learn something, they retained that learning over the long term. They also found that older dogs were better at logical reasoning and staying focused on the task at hand.

While almost every dog trainer agrees it's better to start training your dog early in his development, the best time to start training is right now.

Puppies on the other hand have their own set of unique challenges when it comes to training. One of the biggest problems you'll encounter when training your puppy is his limited attention span and how easily he will become distracted. Regardless of his wondering attention, it's still a good idea to begin teaching your puppy simple commands from the time he is just one month old. It's important you begin training him what you consider acceptable behavior as soon as possible to avoid a bad behavior from becoming a habit. This is not to say that adult dogs cannot be re-trained of bad behaviors, but it will certainly take more time and patience.

Overcoming your pup's short attention span can often be handled with a few correctly-timed dog treats. If the treat is tasty enough, you are bound to get even the most distracted of pups to pay attention while also encouraging him to learn in the process. It is quite easy to teach a puppy the "sit" command when there is a tasty treat on the line. And just by teaching him this most simplest of commands, you will kick-start your entire training program because now he's learned what the reward process is all about. Once he understands the process of command and reward, it will make any future training that much easier.

The easiest way to teach the "sit" command is by holding a treat slightly above your pup's head, making him look up at what you are holding. Don't allow him to jump for the treat. Instead, dangle the treat over his current line of sight. Most dogs trying to follow the morsel of food with their eyes will automatically sit down and raise their heads back to see what is hanging over them. Without even realizing it, your pet will have followed your instruction to sit. And as soon as he does, quickly give him the treat and let out an encouraging, "good dog!" Your pup will know he did good and want to repeat it for both the treat and the praise.

This simple trick should be taught very early on in your dog's training and can be used as the key to unlock the capacity to learn new skill sets. But regardless of what skills you decide to teach your puppy, remember the most valuable part of training is the confidence that it will foster as he grows into an adult.

A Well-Trained Dog Is A Confident Dog

Training your dog not only teaches him good behavior but it also builds a strong sense of self-confidence which is essential to his overall development and well-being. A confident dog is a social dog that is fully adapted to his environment. Dogs with low confidence on the other hand, are usually insecure and anxious. When you see a dog that constantly has his "tail between its legs", it's often a sign that he is both fearful and has low self-esteem. Low self-esteem dogs usually have major behavioral issues.

Building confidence in your pup can be accomplished by giving him the structure he needs to feel more secure. Dogs naturally want to follow a leader and will equate their own self-worth with how well they fit in with the pack. Learning to follow commands from their human "pack leader" early on will give your pup a better sense of belonging later in life.

Final Training Thoughts..

Training your dog or puppy can be a lot of work so it's understandable that you are going to make some mistakes along the way, especially if you have been given poor advice in the past. You should also expect that you will experience some training setbacks that will cause you frustration to the point where you may feel like giving up. Don't.

It will be all be well worth your effort in the long run. You will finally be able to enjoy the perks of your new best friend rather than dealing with his poor behavior all day. Not only will you have more free time because you'll be spending less time cleaning up messes and replacing damaged items, but you'll also feel less stress knowing you can count on your dog to be well-behaved.

I hope that you will take a step back after reading this book and reevaluate some your previous training techniques and their effectiveness. Start thinking of how you can improve your pet's training by incorporating some of these positive training techniques. I promise you, the benefits of having a properly trained dog are plentiful and will leave you thrilled with your new found relationship with man's best friend.

And if there is one thing I would like to impress upon you before you close the covers to this book, it's to please use *positive reinforcement techniques as much as possible.* Positive reinforcement dog training is not only highly effective, it also helps build confidence and strong bonds between a dog and his owner. No dog should have to live in fear of making mistakes.

While there are no shortage of trainers out there who will assert that negative training is necessary. I assure you, it's not. Negative training can result in your pet's distrust. It can also result in long term behavioral problems down the road. Once your dog's trust is violated, it may be a hard thing to win back. The best thing that you can do is to not put yourself in that position. Always train with love and kindness in mind.

Finally, if you enjoyed this book, please take some time to post a review on AMAZON. Remember, reducing the number of dogs in shelters begins with the very first day we bring our new dog or puppy home so let's get the word out.

Kenny P.

Made in the USA
Las Vegas, NV
24 July 2023

75178002R00066